THE VILLA PREMIER YEARS
1992-2010

THE VILLA PREMIER YEARS 1992-2010

A fan's view from a fan

by Steve Brookes

www.villa4lifebooks.co.uk

First published in 2010

This book is copyright under the Berne Convention. All rights are reserved. Apart from any fair dealing for the purpose of private study, research, criticism or review, as permitted under the Copyright Act, 1956, no part of this publication may be reproduced, stored in a retrieval system, or transmitted, in any form or by any means, electronic, electrical, chemical, mechanical, optical, photocopying, recording or otherwise, without the prior permission of the copyright owner. Enquiries should be sent to the publishers at the undermentioned address:

EMPIRE PUBLICATIONS
1 Newton Street, Manchester M1 1HW
© Steve Brookes 2010

ISBN: 1901746 623 - 9781901746624

Cover design and layout: Ashley Shaw

Printed in Great Britain by

This book is dedicated to Christopher Priest
11th March 1982 - 20th April 2008
'The Big Friendly Giant'

CONTENTS

FOREWORD by Julian Joachim 7

OWNERS
    DOUG ELLIS PROFILE 13
    RANDOLF D LERNER PROFILE 15

TEAM MANAGERS
    1. RON ATKINSON 19
    2. BRIAN LITTLE 21
    3. JOHN GREGORY 23
    4. GRAHAM TAYLOR 25
    5. DAVID O'LEARY 27
    6. MARTIN O'NEILL 31

TOP 23 PLAYER PROFILES
    1. PAUL MCGRATH 38
    2. IAN TAYLOR 40
    3. DEAN SAUNDERS 42
    4. PAUL MERSON 44
    5. MARTIN LAURSEN 46
    6. ASHLEY YOUNG 48
    7. DWIGHT YORKE 50
    8. GARETH BARRY 52
    9. STEVE STAUNTON 54
    10. DION DUBLIN 56
    11. THOMAS HITZLESPERGER 59
    12. SHAUN TEALE 61
    13. DALIAN ATKINSON 63
    14. NOLBERTO SOLANO 65
    15. TONY DALEY 67
    16. UGO EHIOGU 69
    17. OLOF MELLBERG 71
    18. GABRIEL AGBONLAHOR 73
    19. MARK BOSNICH 76
    20. GARETH SOUTHGATE 78
    21. GORDON SIDNEY COWANS 80

22.	PHILIP GEOFFREY KING	82
23.	JAMES MILNER	84

STATS

1.	ASTON VILLA HISTORY	88
2.	CLUB BACKGROUND	89
2.	CLUB HONOURS	91
3.	VILLA v. BLUES ALL TIME HEAD TO HEAD	92
4.	SQUAD LISTS 1992 - 2010	96
5.	SEASON-BY-SEASON: FIXTURES & RESULTS, BEST RESULTS & LEAGUE TABLES	

1992/93	118
1993/94	121
1994/95	123
1995/96	127
1996/97	130
1997/98	133
1998/99	135
1999/2000	139
2000/01	142
2001/02	145
2002/03	148
2003/04	151
2004/05	154
2005/06	157
2006/07	160
2007/08	163
2008/09	165
A SELECTION OF PREMIER LEAGUE GAMES	169
FIRST GAMES OF EVERY SEASON	182
RESULTS AGAINST ALL MIDLAND OPPOSITION	182

MY VILLA BEST XI 185

FOREWORD

Hi to all you Villa fans,

I played for Aston Villa from 1996 – 2001, I remember my time fondly there and I played in a lot of very important games. The atmosphere at Villa Park was one of the best I have known, I still follow the Villa closely. It was Brian Little that signed me and we had a very good squad, we had just won the Coca Cola Cup and the Team spirit in the team was second to none.

This is a very well written book and a lot of detail has gone in to it, it brings back a hell of a lot of memories and some of the great players I played with. This book includes all the history of the Premier League, Superbly researched, there are a lot of magical moments in there. I am also very pleased that Aston Villa are competing in the Carling Cup Final v Manchester United at Wembley.

Villa have really changed a lot since I was there with Randy Lerner Taking over as chairman and they really have a great manager now in Martin O'Neill who I worked under myself. I can see Villa eventually breaking the Top 4 and being involved in a lot more Cup Finals and progressing in Europe also.

The future is very bright for Villa, and I will enjoy following them in the future.

All the Best

Julian Joachim

ACKNOWLEDGEMENTS

I cannot actually remember the day the thought came to me to write this book, but when I thought of Aston Villa's Premier League Years.

I started to think about all the players. Including the key players, the fans favourites and the forgotten players. The list of every player who has played for us since 1992 is towards the back of the book and I must say some of the names really will bring back memories.

I thought about the managers, games, and different stats that would interest the majority of villa fans. It's a shame when villa won the European cup in 1982 I was not born until August that year, but I have so many wonderful memories including going to Wembley. I would like to thank a number of people for helping me, supporting me, promoting my book and encouraging me along the way including Ashley Shaw, David Chant, Stacey Fellows, Duncan Kemp, Sue Montgomery, Philip Montgomery, John Morris, Max wall, Devon Lions, Simon Staples, Viv Deeprose, and Andrew Webster.

I'm so sorry if I have forgotten to mention anyone who contributed to this publication. It's been such a pleasure networking with Villa fans, getting involved in a number of things, its nice to know villa really is a big family, the greatest well run club in the world.

Steve Brookes

PS. In January we went through to the Carling Cup Final 2010 where we will play Man United I am so chuffed. The Villa Park semi against Blackburn looked amazing with all the free flags - the atmosphere was awesome. It's up there with the Tranmere and Inter games in the 90's for me...

INTRODUCTION

My first Aston Villa game was in 1988 against Oldham Athletic when I was 6, Cyrille Regis won the game for us 1-0 with I think minutes to spare.

I was hooked from that moment, and I got a season ticket with my father, but when I was 12 I started to go with friends and always in the Holte End. We have the best loudest support in the country home and away, I love going to the away games and especially recently going to Prague and Hamburg and hopefully many more to come.

There is normally a lot of us drinking in the Aston Social before and after games, the atmosphere is brilliant.

We have had so many great players down the years which feature in this book and I'm sure you will all agree with my top 23 players. We have some great times ahead now, I think we have all suffered in the past but, the future is bright... the future is claret and blue.

I really believe Martin O'Neill and Randolph Lerner is the best partnership we could have, Randy really does care about the club and has been very generous, and Martin is one of the best managers in Europe. I really hope they stay together for the next 10 years at least and I can really see us conquering Europe and getting into in the Top 4 in the league.

Hope you all enjoy this book,
All the Best and
UP THE VILLA !!!!!

Steve Brookes
www.villa4lifebooks.co.uk

OWNER PROFILES

DOUG ELLIS

Born: Herbert Doug Ellis
D.O.B: 3 January 1924
Birth Place: Hooton, Cheshire, England
Nationality British
Other names 'Deadly Doug'
Occupation: President Emeritus
(Life President) of Aston Villa

Ellis began life in a poor family with a widowed mother. Before he was 40, he had become a millionaire by pioneering package holidays to Spain.

Aston Villa

Ellis was a controversial chairman and major shareholder of Aston Villa for two separate spells; the first being from 1968 to 1975. Ellis was replaced as chairman and finally ousted from the board in 1979. During his absence Aston Villa enjoyed its greatest period of success in modern times, winning the Football League title in 1981 and the European Cup in 1982 - some say this was not coincidental!

Ellis returned as chairman in 1982 and remained there until selling to Randy Lerner in 2006. Most fans blame him for the decline of the club after the European Cup victory in 1981/2. Within five years the club was relegated from the top flight, with many of the European Cup-winning team being sold to other teams, although it can be argued that this was due to large debts built up during the previous regime. In 1996 Doug Ellis owned 47 percent of Aston Villa. In May 1997 the club floated on the stock market with a valuation of £126m. Ellis sold a number of his shares at flotation, reducing his shareholding to around one-third of the total shares. It is reported that Ellis made £4m from this deal, although the flotation also raised funds to pay for the construction of the new Trinity Road Stand and for the £7m transfer of Stan Collymore from Liverpool, among others. Since the flotation, the club's share price had fallen by almost 90%.

Some Villa fans were disappointed with the destruction of the 1920s Trinity Road stand ("the St Pancras of football", as a *Sunday Times* reporter called it in 1960), which many believe should have been a listed building. The replacement, although state of the art, never had the grandeur of the original.

Ellis was reported to be the first football club director to pay himself a salary (in 2005 it was £290,000 after a 12% increase from the previous year) when it was made legal by The Football Association in the early 1980s. Along with this, his professed love of Aston Villa Football Club has been questioned in light of the fact that he has served on the Boards of Villa's arch-rivals Birmingham City, Derby County and Wolverhampton Wanderers (as Chairman).

In 2004, at the age of 80 and suffering from prostate cancer, Ellis agreed to relinquish some of his control of the club by appointing Bruce Langham as chief executive. Langham resigned in May 2005, reportedly after a disagreement with Ellis.

In 2005 he was awarded an OBE in the New Year Honours List. Later that year he underwent a heart bypass operation and, after a three-month absence, returned to his role at Villa Park soon after the start of the 2005/2006 season.

On 14 August 2006, it was announced that Ellis had agreed to sell the club to American billionaire, Randy Lerner in a deal worth £63 million. Ellis stood aside when the takeover was completed on 19 September 2006, becoming a President Emeritus (Life President) of the club. Doug received an honorary degree from Aston University in July 2007(the campus of which is located 2 miles north of Villa Park in the centre of Birmingham).

Supporters and former club managers criticised Ellis's alleged lack of ambition, noting that the club often struggled to bring in top players. Ellis responded that his approach had always been one of financial prudence, helping to avoid the fate of big-borrowing clubs such as Leeds United. Under John Gregory the club had been one of the biggest spenders in the Premier League, but Gregory always wanted 2-3 more players.

In his autobiography Ellis claims to have invented the Bicycle Kick, despite the fact that he has never actually played football.

There were several supporter-led campaigns for Ellis to stand down from his position, and in his final years at the club a number of interested parties made unsuccessful attempts to buy his stake in the club.

Doug has three sons and has been married to Heidi Marie since 1963. He is reportedly worth around £10,000,000, much of it arising from selling off his Aston Villa shares.

*   *   *

RANDOLPH D LERNER

Born February 21, 1962
Place of Birth: Brooklyn, New York, USA
Occupation: Owner of the Cleveland Browns, Chairman of Aston Villa F.C
Net worth: $1.5 billion (2008)
Spouse(s): Lara Lerner
Children: 3

Lerner has been the owner of the American football team, the Cleveland Browns, of the National Football League (NFL) since October 2002, and the Chairman of Aston Villa Football Club of Birmingham, England since 2006. His personal fortune is estimated at over $1.5 billion in 2008.

Lerner graduated from Columbia University in 1984, spending 1983 at Clare College in Cambridge, England. During his time at Cambridge Lerner followed English football (soccer), taking an interest in three teams: Arsenal, Fulham and Aston Villa. He graduated from Columbia Law School and is a member of the New York and District of Columbia Bar Associations. Prior to entering the business world, he worked as a lawyer in New York City.

Although he had grown up in the United States, with a father who had been involved with the original Cleveland Browns franchise under Art Modell, Lerner's interest in England's top flight endured long after he had returned to the States. He eventually added Aston Villa to his list of investments, becoming the second American owner of a Premiership club in 2006 - the first being Malcolm Glazer, who purchased the majority share of Manchester United in 2005. Since then Liverpool FC has also had American investment in the shape of George Gillett and Tom Hicks.

Lerner's business career began at the Progressive Corporation as an investment analyst. In 1991, he started an independent investment firm with Progressive capital called Securities Advisors, Inc. (SAI), which he owned and managed until 2001. SAI initially specialized in arbitrage before shifting its focus to equity investing.

In 1993, Lerner became a director at MBNA, a company in which his father was founder and builder, and continued to lead until his father's death at which time he became company chairman.

CLEVELAND BROWNS

Control of the Browns was given to Lerner, when his father, Al Lerner died in October 2002 - four years to the day after he was awarded the new Browns franchise. He also serves as a member of the National Football League's Business Ventures Committee. Lerner has generally been a low key owner since assuming control of the franchise.

ASTON VILLA

On 24 July 2006 it was reported that Randy Lerner intended to purchase English Premiership association football club Aston Villa F.C. following a statement from Cleveland Browns management indicating Lerner was pursuing business interests in the United Kingdom. Lerner pulled out of the bid to buy Aston Villa two days later after talks with the club chairman Doug Ellis broke down but the following day reports emerged that Lerner might still make a formal £64 million bid for the club.

On 14 August 2006 it was confirmed that Lerner had reached an agreement of £62.6 million with Aston Villa for a takeover of the club. The statement to the London Stock Exchange confirmed that 60% of the club's shares, including the 39% stake of Doug Ellis had been sold to Lerner, beating competition from consortia led by Michael Neville, Nicholas Padfield QC, and Athole Still. At this stage, the sale still awaited the approval of the shareholders of Aston Villa, although it was expected to be approved without a hitch.

On 25 August, the LSE announced that Lerner had secured 59.69% of Villa shares, making him the majority shareholder. He also appointed himself Chairman of the club.

The *BBC* reported on 5 September 2006 that Lerner had now moved closer to taking full control of the club, after increasing his share to 85.5%.

By the time that the September 18 1pm deadline had been reached RAL had acceptance of 89.69% of the share. Due to the acceptance only being 0.31% below the conditional limit, RAL accepted it and made the bid unconditional. On September 19 2006 Aston Villa PLC executive Chairman Doug Ellis and his board resigned, to be replaced by Randy Lerner as Chairman and General Charles C.Krulak, Bob Kain and Michael Martin as non-executive directors.

Randy Lerner has supported the National Portrait Gallery since 2002. On January 23, 2008 it was announced that he had donated £5 million to the gallery, the largest single donation that it has ever received. In recognition the ground floor galleries will be named "The Lerner Galleries".

For the 2008/2009 season, Aston Villa will forego traditional shirt sponsorship, which is nowadays a very lucrative sponsorship, by instead wearing on their shirts the name of a local children's hospice, Acorns.

MANAGER PROFILES

1. Ron Atkinson
2. Brian Little
3. John Gregory
4. Graham Taylor
5. David O'leary
6. Martin O'neill Obe

RON ATKINSON

Full name: Ronald Franklin Atkinson
Date of birth: 18 March 1939
Place of birth: Liverpool, England
Playing position: Wing half (retired)

Senior clubs
Years   Club   Apps Goals
1959–1971   Oxford United   383   14

Teams managed
1971–1974 Kettering Town
1974–1978 Cambridge United
1978–1981 West Bromwich Albion
1981–1986 Manchester United
1987–1988 West Bromwich Albion
1988–1989 Atlético Madrid
1989–1991 Sheffield Wednesday
1991–1994 Aston Villa
1995–1996 Coventry City
1997–1998 Sheffield Wednesday
1999 Nottingham Forest
2006 Peterborough United (caretaker)

Ronald Franklin Atkinson universally known as "Big Ron" and (earlier in his managerial career) "Bojangles" was born on 18 March 1939. In recent years he has become one of Britain's best-known football pundits. He is perhaps most famous for his idiosyncratic turns of phrase: his utterances have become known as "Big-Ronisms" or "Ronglish" - although in recent times, he has also attracted a lot of controversy over a racist comment broadcast on a TV sports show when he believed he was off the air.

Ron Atkinson, who was born in Liverpool but moved to Birmingham a few weeks after his birth, was originally signed by Villa at the age of 17, but never played a first-team match for them and was transferred to Oxford United in the close season of 1959 on a free transfer. There he played with his younger brother Graham Atkinson. He went on to make over 500 appearances as a wing-half for the club, earning the nickname "The Tank" and scored a total of 14 goals. He was Oxford's captain through their rise from the Southern League to the Second Division, achieved in just six years, from 1962 to 1968. He was the first man to captain a club from the Southern League through three divisions of the Football League.

He offended some Sheffield Wednesday fans by saying on 31 May 1991 that he would be staying as manager but a week later leaving to become Villa manager.

Taking over from Dr Jozef Venglos, he led Villa to 2nd place in the inaugural FA Premier League season in 1992/93 and to victory in the League Cup in 1994. Despite leading Villa to their first major success since lifting the European Cup, a mutual dislike between chairman Doug Ellis and Ron that developed from 1992, inevitably resulted in him being sacked. Big Ron was sacked on November 10 1994 following a 4-3 defeat at the hands of Wimbledon - three days after Ellis had given Ron a 'vote of confidence' in the media, stating that Ron was one of England's top three football managers. Shortly after the Villa sacking, he became manager at Coventry City replacing Phil Neal.

Atkinson is famous for a number of remarkable quotes. A number of example are: 'They scored too early.'; 'Apart from picking the ball out of the net, he hasn't had to make a save.' ; 'That's not the type of header you want to see your defender make, with his hand.' ; 'You don't want to be giving away free kicks in the penalty area'.

BRIAN LITTLE

Date of birth: 25 November 1953
Place of birth: Horden, England
Playing position: Forward

SENIOR CLUBS
Years	Club	Apps	Goals
1970–79	Aston Villa	247	60

TEAMS MANAGED
1986 Wolverhampton Wanderers
1989–1991 Darlington
1991–1994 Leicester City
1994–1998 Aston Villa
1998–1999 Stoke City
1999–2000 West Bromwich Albion
2000–2002 Hull City
2003–2006 Tranmere Rovers
2007–2008 Wrexham

PLAYING CAREER

In 1970 Little signed for Villa who had just been relegated to the Third Division for the first time in their history. He progressed through the youth ranks, winning an FA Youth Cup winners' medal along the way. He made 247 appearances for the club and scored 60 goals, and made one full international appearance for England in 1975.

He was part of Villa's League Cup winning teams of 1975 & 1977 as well as helping the club climb from the Third to the First Division in the early part of the decade.

His playing career came to a halt in 1979 when he retired at the age of 26 due to a knee injury. The injury was discovered when Little was undergoing a medical at Villa's local rivals Birmingham City. This meant his intended transfer there was cancelled. He was a flamboyant forward who formed a particularly prolific partnership with Andy Gray, and is regarded as an all-time great at Villa Park.

In November 1994 Little returned to Aston Villa to replace Ron

Atkinson. Leicester's first Premier League season was difficult and they were relegated in second from bottom place, with just six league wins all season.

Eighteen months earlier, Villa had finished runners-up in the first Premier League. When Little arrived they were at the foot of the division. Significant players like Nigel Spink, Earl Barrett, Shaun Teale, Ray Houghton, Garry Parker, Dalian Atkinson and Dean Saunders were starting to age. A 1–1 draw with relegated Norwich City on the last day of the season meant that Little was successful in his bid to keep Villa in the Premiership.

In place of the fading stars came a whole set of new players in the Villa line-up. Young players such as Mark Bosnich and Ugo Ehiogu were now getting more first team chances, but Villa also made a large number of new signings between November 94 and August 95, including Gary Charles, Ian Taylor, Mark Draper and Savo Miloševic. The new look Villa team gelled well, and 1995–96 was the most successful season at Villa Park in years. The club finished 4th in the Premiership, reached the FA Cup semi-finals and won the Coca-Cola Cup with a 3–0 win over Leeds at Wembley. Trinidad and Tobago striker Dwight Yorke had now firmly established himself as a world-class goalscorer.

Villa qualified for the 1996–97 UEFA Cup and although they were knocked out at the first stage by Swedish part-timers Helsingborg, they qualified for the 1997–98 competition after finishing 5th in the Premiership.

In February 1998, Brian Little resigned after just over three years as Aston Villa manager, with the club in the bottom half of the Premiership. But the club's next manager John Gregory turned results around and they finished high enough for a UEFA Cup place.

JOHN GREGORY

Full name : John Charles Gregory
Date of birth: May 11, 1954
Place of birth: Scunthorpe, England
Playing position: Midfielder

SENIOR CLUBS

Years	Club	Apps	Gls
1972–1977	Northampton Town	187	8
1977–1979	Aston Villa	65	10
1979–1981	Brighton & Hove Albion	72	7
1981–1985	Queens Park Rangers	161	36
1985–1988	Derby County	103	22
1990	Plymouth Argyle	3	0
1990	Bolton Wanderers	7	0
	Total	**598**	**83**

TEAMS MANAGED
1989–1990 Portsmouth
1990   Plymouth Argyle
1996–1998 Wycombe Wanderers
1998–2002 Aston Villa
2002–2003 Derby County
2006–2007 Queens Park Rangers

Gregory previously managed Portsmouth, Plymouth Argyle, Wycombe Wanderers, Aston Villa, Derby County and Queens Park Rangers. A versatile midfielder who started his career at Northampton Town and later played for Brighton & Hove Albion, Queens Park Rangers, Derby County and Villa. He won six caps for England.

He worked under Little on the coaching staff at Leicester City (1991-1994) and Aston Villa (1994-96) before moving back into management with Wycombe Wanderers in September 96.

Wycombe were performing well in February 1998 when Gregory quit to take the manager's job back at Aston Villa. He helped improve

Villa's league form during the final 3 months of the 1997-98 season and they qualified for the UEFA Cup.

Halfway through the 1998-99 season Villa were Premiership leaders but a slump in form saw the club eventually finish sixth in the final table and miss out on a European place.

Villa reached the FA Cup final in 2000 but lost to Chelsea. Gregory finally quit in Jan 2002, with Villa going on to finish 8th that season.

Gregory's spell at Villa is also notable as he became the last manager to field an all English starting 11 in the Premiership until Steve McClaren's Middlesbrough did the same against Fulham on May 7, 2006.

GRAHAM TAYLOR

Date of birth: 15 September 1944
Place of birth: Worksop, Nottinghamshire.

SENIOR CLUBS

Years	Club		Apps	Goals
1962-1968	Grimsby Town		189	2
1968-1972	Lincoln City		150	1
		Total	339	3

TEAMS MANAGED
1972-1977 Lincoln City
1977-1987 Watford
1987-1990 Aston Villa
1990-1993 England
1994-1995 Wolverhampton Wanderers
1996 Watford
1997-2001 Watford
2002-2003 Aston Villa

Graham Taylor OBE (born 15 September 1944, Worksop, Nottinghamshire) is best known as the manager of the England national team between 1990 and 1993. He came to prominence as manager of Watford, a club he took from the Fourth Division to the First in the space of 5 years.

Taylor grew up in the industrial steel town of Scunthorpe, North Lincolnshire, a town with which he still has many connections and regards as his hometown. The son of a sports journalist with the *Scunthorpe Evening Telegraph*, Graham found his love of the beautiful game in the stands of the "Old Showground" watching Scunthorpe United, a team he still supports and is often seen at many home matches.

The style of football his teams played was often criticised by purists as being focused on the 'long ball' style of getting the ball quickly to physically powerful forwards, although he also liked to play with skillful wingers, who could beat defenders, hit the byline and produce dangerous crosses into the opposition's penalty area. In this respect, John Barnes was perhaps the archetypal Taylor player.

Although viewed as being aesthetically unattractive by the opposition, Taylor's style proved incredibly successful in terms of club football, although less so when applied to the more composed pace and sophisticated tactics of international football.

His first spell at Aston Villa brought the club to runners-up spot in the First Division in 1990 after which he was appointed England boss. His second spell during the 2002-03 season wasn't as successful...

DAVID O'LEARY

Full name: David Anthony O'Leary
Date of birth: May 2, 1958
Place of birth: Stoke Newington, London, England
Playing position: Centre back (retired)

SENIOR CLUBS

Years	Club	Apps	Goals
1975-1993	Arsenal	558	11
1993-1995	Leeds United	12	0
	Total	570	11

NATIONAL TEAM

1993-1993	Republic of Ireland	68	1

TEAMS MANAGED

1998-2002 Leeds United
2003-2006 Aston Villa

David Anthony O'Leary is currently without a job, after leaving his position as manager of Aston Villa in July 2006. He made his managerial name at Leeds United, guiding the Yorkshire club to the upper echelons of the Premiership and to a Champions League semi-final. The majority of his playing career (19 years) was spent as a defender at Arsenal. He currently lives in the small village of Sicklinghall, near Harrogate, North Yorkshire.

O'Leary was born in Stoke Newington, London on May 2, 1958 and moved to live in Dublin at the age of three. His father was born in Ireland and O'Leary opted to play for the Republic.

O'Leary signed for Arsenal as an apprentice in 1973. He soon progressed through the ranks at Highbury, playing in the reserves at the age of 16. He made his debut for Arsenal against Burnley on August 16, 1975, and despite being only 17, went on to make 30 appearances that season. For the next 10 years he was ever-present in the Arsenal side, playing more than 40 matches a season (except for 1980-81, where he was injured and only played 27).

A calm and collected centre half, O'Leary was noted for his good positioning and elegant style of play. He was nicknamed by Arsenal fans "Spider" because of his long legs intercepting passes from the opposition. He won his first major honour with Arsenal when he played in their 3-2 win over Manchester United in the 1979 FA Cup final. He also played in the 1978 and 1980 Cup finals, and the 1980 Cup Winners' Cup final, all of which Arsenal lost. In 1982 O'Leary became club captain, but reliniquished teh armband to Graham Rix 18 months later.

O'Leary broke numerous appearance records at Arsenal; he was the youngest person to reach the 100 and 200 match milestones, and he made his 400th appearance while still only 26. He passed George Armstrong's all-time record of 621 first-team games in November 1989. By this time, O'Leary was no longer automatic first choice (with the partnership of Tony Adams and Steve Bould at the centre of George Graham's defence), but he still turned in over 20 appearances as Arsenal won the 1988-89 First Division title.

O'Leary won another League title in 1991 and an FA Cup and League Cup double in 1993, though by this time he was mainly used as a sub. He holds Arsenal's all-time record for appearances, with 722 first-team games, and over 1000 games at all levels, in a twenty-year long association with the club.

Manager of Aston Villa

O'Leary was linked with various other vacant manager's jobs throughout the 2002-03 season. He was hot favourite to become manager of Sunderland when Peter Reid was sacked in October and again when Howard Wilkinson was sacked in March. But O'Leary remained out of work until June 2003 when he was appointed manager of Villa.

By the beginning of November 2003, Aston Villa were hovering just above the relegation zone. O'Leary managed to push a limited squad to perform successfully and consistently, led by the revitalised Colombian striker Juan Pablo Angel, and by the final weeks of the season they were in with a real chance of a European competition qualification place. In the end they had to settle for sixth place - this season one place too low for European qualification due to Millwall's

FA Cup final appearance and Middlesbrough's Worthington Cup triumph. It was still a remarkable achievement from O'Leary, who had to deal with a downsized first team squad and a lack of transfer funds, and although some felt that Villa had overachieved in reaching 6th place, it was still creditable, with the club improving 10 places and now fans had some much needed optimism. The new found form of Angel, neglected under previous manager Graham Taylor, also saw Villa possess a dangerous weapon for the next season.

2004-05

The 2004/05 season was somewhat disappointing, as Villa finished tenth in the league, a drop from the previous season, despite often giving performances suggesting that they could improve on the previous season's achievement. Despite this, O'Leary once again avoided any risk of relegation and signed AC Milan's international defender Martin Laursen, the new Paul McGrath, highly rated Chelsea prodigy Carlton Cole and acclaimed French midfielder Mathieu Berson, while still restriced by a tight budget imposed by chairman Doug Ellis. Although there were some criticisms of his relationship with fans and his motivational skills, O'Leary insured that there would be no scares like those suffered under Taylor's disastrous second era in charge. There was also much encouragement as a result of the return to form of the outcast Lee Hendrie and the occasionally erratic Nolberto Solano, which seemed to dispel some doubt over his motivational skills.

2005-06

Despite six summer acquisitions including Milan Baroš and Kevin Phillips who added more quality to the squad, the 2005-06 season brought a disappointing turn for the worse for O'Leary. Injuries and suspensions decimated the squad, with only one fit centre back (Liam Ridgewell) available for selection at one point. Increasingly under-fire from fans and media alike, the season saw a highly embarrassing League Cup exit via a 0-3 defeat to League One side Doncaster Rovers. A series of poor results saw Villa hovering dangerously above the relegation zone going into December, with just 17 points from 17 games.

However an improved winter period saw them move slightly up the league, with encouraging victories over Everton (4-0), Middlesbrough (4-0) and a well-earned point against runaway champions Chelsea. In the end, Villa finished a disappointing 16th, just two places above the relegation zone. Following the relegation of local rivals Birmingham City and West Bromwich Albion, Villa were the only Midlands side playing Premiership football in 2006-07.

A storm broke surrounding David O'Leary and Villa on 14 July 2006 when a press release from the Villa players criticised Ellis and his ownership of Villa. The media furore finally came to a head when on 19 July 2006, O'Leary's contract as Aston Villa manager was terminated by mutual consent. As it happened, Ellis sold the club within a few months to Randy Lerner, and Martin O'Neill was appointed as manager.

MARTIN O'NEILL, OBE

Full name: Martin Hugh Michael O'Neill
Date of birth: 1 March 1952
Place of birth: Kilrea, Northern Ireland
Playing position: Midfielder

SENIOR CLUBS

Years	Club	Apps	Goals
1971	Distillery F.C		
1971–1981	Nottingham Forest	285	48
1981	Norwich City	11	1
1981–1982	Manchester City	13	0
1982–1983	Norwich City	55	11
1983–1985	Notts County	64	5
	Total	**428**	**65**

NATIONAL TEAM
1971–1984   Northern Ireland

TEAMS MANAGED
1987–1989 Grantham Town
1989 Shepshed Charterhouse
1990–1995 Wycombe Wanderers
1995 Norwich City
1995–2000 Leicester City
2000–2005 Glasgow Celtic
2006– Aston Villa

Martin Hugh Michael O'Neill, OBE, (born 1 March 1952 in Kilrea, Northern Ireland) has previously managed Wycombe Wanderers, Norwich City, Leicester City and Glasgow Celtic and is currently manager of Aston Villa. O'Neill is perhaps best known for his time as Celtic manager between 2000 and 2005 when he led the club to three Scottish Premier League titles and the 2003 UEFA Cup Final in Seville.

He also played Gaelic football as a youth, winning the MacRory Cup in 1970 with St. Malachy's College in Belfast. He attended St.

Malachy's College with Irish chef Eamonn Ó'Catháin. While at St. Malachy's, he first came to public attention as a football player with local side Distillery F.C.. This breached the Gaelic Athletic Association prohibition on gaelic footballers' playing "foreign sports", and the resulting disputes raised O'Neill's profile. After completing his education at St. Columb's College, Derry, he began a degree in law at the Queen's University of Belfast. While at Distillery F.C., he won the Irish Cup in 1971 scoring twice in the final. He also scored against FC Barcelona in the UEFA Cup Winners' Cup in a 3-1 home defeat in September 1971. It was during this period he was spotted by a scout for Nottingham Forest F.C., for whom he signed in 1971, quitting his studies.

PLAYING CAREER

Before playing for Distillery in the Irish League, O'Neill played for the South Belfast side Rosario were he progressed greatly and is the clubs most notable player to date. O'Neill progressed slowly as a player until the legendary Brian Clough arrived at the City Ground as manager in 1975 and made him a key part of his midfield. O'Neill went on to play an integral role in Forest's golden era, in which they gained promotion to the top flight, then won the League and League Cup in 1978, followed by further League Cup success a year later and the first of two European Cup triumphs. O'Neill was a regular for his country, captaining the Northern Ireland side at a memorable 1982 FIFA World Cup in Spain, which included defeating the host nation in Valencia. He played 62 times and scored 8 goals for Northern Ireland. At club level he also played for Norwich City F.C., Manchester City F.C. and Notts County F.C. before retiring.

MANAGERIAL CAREER

After his playing career, O'Neill began a sensational career in football management, initially at Grantham Town in 1987. After a brief spell at the helm of Shepshed Charterhouse, he managed non-league Wycombe Wanderers, and took them into the Football League as Conference champions in 1993. They had narrowly missed out on promotion the previous year after a two-horse race with Colchester United.

Norwich City

He became manager of Norwich City in the summer of 1995, but left the club in December of that year due to differences with club chairman Robert Chase.

Leicester City

He joined Leicester City immediately after leaving Norwich City. After a difficult start he achieved great success at the club, gaining promotion via the play-offs to the Premiership in the same season as joining the club. Leicester finished in the top half of the Premiership in every season O'Neill was manager. They also won the Football League Cup in 1997 and 2000, as well as reaching the 1999 final of the competition. They finished ninth in 1997, tenth in 1998 and 1999, and eighth in 2000. The two League Cup triumphs saw them qualify for the UEFA Cup each time, though both campaigns were short-lived.

During his time at Leicester, O'Neill held talks to become manager of Leeds United but declined the job after thousands of supporters held up placards saying "Don't go Martin!" in an effort to make him stay.

Celtic

O'Neill eventually left Leicester on 1 June 2000, taking over from the team of John Barnes and Kenny Dalglish to become manager of Celtic. It was at Celtic that O'Neill gained his nicknames "Martin the Magnificent" and "the Blessed Martin". O'Neill's first Old Firm game ended in a dramatic 6-2 victory for Celtic over Rangers and did much to overturn the psychological advantage previously held by Rangers. In that first season O'Neill's Celtic won the domestic treble. He was also the first Celtic manager to take the team into the revamped Champions League (a feat he managed three times). In the first season in the CL Celtic were eliminated in spite of having 9 points.

Perhaps his greatest achievement was to guide Celtic to the 2003 UEFA Cup Final held in Seville. Celtic lost 3-2 in extra time, to a Porto side coached by Jose Mourinho that went on to win the Champions League a season later. In his five seasons at Celtic Park, O'Neill won three League titles, three Scottish Cups, and a League Cup. He also oversaw a record 7 consecutive victories in Old Firm derbies, and in season 2003-04 Celtic created a British record of 25 consecutive victories. During this time, O'Neill's name was linked with a number of high-profile jobs in England.

On 25 May 2005, Celtic announced that O'Neill was resigning as manager at the end of the 2004/05 season to care for his wife Geraldine, who has lymphoma.

O'Neill's last competitive game in charge of Celtic was the Scottish Cup final 1 – 0 victory over Dundee United on 28 May 2005, decided by an eleventh minute goal by former Villa star Alan Thompson. Celtic had an impressive record under O'Neill, playing 282 games and winning 213, drawing 29 and losing 40.

LEEDS CONTRACT

Revelations in Peter Ridsdale's book 'United We Fall', later confirmed by O'Neill, have shown that he signed a conditional agreement with Ridsdale in January 2003, to leave Celtic and become Leeds United AFC manager. This deal subsequently fell through on the departure of Ridsdale from Leeds, one of the conditions for the deal, and the failure of Ridsdale to remove Terry Venables as manager. O'Neill has since hit out at Ridsdale, describing the agreement as 'full of conditions that hadn't been true' and blaming Celtic's failure to offer a new contact as his reason for the deal.

ASTON VILLA

O'Neill was introduced as Aston Villa manager at a press conference on 4 August 2006 which was my birthday and that was the best birthday present ever as I knew there was no one better to take this wonderful club forward. At the press conference he stated "It's absolutely fantastic to be back and with a club such as this. This is a fantastic challenge. I am well aware of the history of this football club. Trying to restore it to its days of former glory seems a long way away - but why not try? It is nearly 25 years since they won the European Cup but that is the dream."

Villa's form improved substantially following O'Neill's appointment. They had the longest unbeaten start of any Premiership side in 2006-07 (9 games), not losing a league game until 28 October.

Villa suffered a mid-season slump but recovered late in the season, winning their three away games in April to end the season how it began with a run of 9 unbeaten fixtures. For this O'Neill scooped the Barclays Manager of the Month for April.

After the World Cup, Aston Villa's owner Randy Lerner said that he would not stop O'Neill from leaving Villa if offered the job of England manager, because he respects that it is a very prestigious position. O'Neill later dismissed the reports, calling them "unfair speculation".

The 2007-08 season was a fantastic season for O'Neill and Aston Villa as they just missed out on a UEFA Cup spot on the final day of the season but qualified for the InterToto Cup by finshing 6th. They also scored 71 goals, (Villa's best ever tally in the Premier League and best since winning the title in 1981), gained 60 points which was Villa's highest points tally since the 1996-97 season, were the 3rd highest goalscorers and were praised for their well-organised, counter-attacking football, something associated with O'Neill's Leicester City and Celtic teams.

Outside football

Despite never completing his degree, O'Neill remains a keen follower of criminology and attended some of Britain's most infamous trials, including those of the Yorkshire Ripper, Rosemary West and more recently the re-trial of Barry Bulsara. His fascination began with the James Hanratty case of 1961.

Martin O'Neill was awarded an OBE for services to sport in 2004. In 2002, Norwich supporters voted him into the club's Hall of Fame.

Personal life

Martin O'Neill is married to Geraldine. The couple live in Oxfordshire, and have two daughters, Aisling and Alana

Martin O'Neill's managerial career

Team	From	To	Games	Won	Lost	Drawn
CELTIC	01-06-2000	31-05-2005	282	213	40	29
LEICESTER	21-12-1995	01-06-2000	223	85	70	68
NORWICH	13-06-1995	17-11-1995	20	9	4	7
WYCOMBE	01-08-1990	13-06-1995	112	52	28	32

THE VILLA PREMIER YEARS - 1992-2010

Villa just missed out on a top 4 place at the end of the 2008/09 season but in January 2010 they lay 6th and qualified for the Final of the Carling Cup following an amazing 6-4 win over Blackburn at a memorable night at Villa Park.

PLAYER PROFILES

1. Paul McGrath
2. Ian Taylor
3. Dean Saunders
4. Paul Merson
5. Martin Laursen
6. Ashley Young
7. Dwight Yorke
8. Gareth Barry
9. Steve Staunton
10. Dion Dublin
11. Thomas Hitzlesperger
12. Shaun Teale
13. Dalian Atkinson
14. Nolberto Solano
15. Tony Daley
16. Ugo Ehiogu
17. Olof Mellberg
18. Gabriel Agbonlahor
19. Mark Bosnich
20. Gareth Southgate
21. Gordon Cowans
22. Phil King
23. James Milner

PAUL "GOD" MCGRATH

Date of birth: 4 December 1959
Place of birth: Ealing, England
Height: 6 ft 2 in
Playing position: Defender
Transfer Cost: £400,000

Senior clubs

Years	Club	App	Gls
1979–1982	St Patrick's Athletic	0	0
1982–1989	Manchester United	163	12
1989–1996	Aston Villa	252	9
1996–1997	Derby County	24	0
1997	Sheffield United (loan)	7	0
1997–1998	Sheffield United	5	0
	Total	**451**	**21**

National team

1985–1997	Republic of Ireland	83	8

Paul played his first game for St Patrick's in a League Cup game with Shamrock Rovers, He was given the nickname "The Black Pearl of Inchicore" and he was awarded the PFAI Player of the Year Award in his first season.

Macca went to Man United, managed by Big Ron in 1982. He won the FA Cup In 1985 where they beat Everton 1–0 and was awarded the Man of the Match.

In my opinion he is one of the best defenders the game has ever seen, it was a shame that several knee injuries stopped Macca from playing much for new United manager Alex Ferguson. His well documented alcohol problems led to a fall out with the United boss and the club, assuming his top flight career was over, offered him a package of £100k and a testimonial. Macca refused, and his former manager Atkinson tried to sign him for Sheffield Wednesday, before Villa's offer was accepted in 1989. It was the start of Paul's beautiful relationship with Aston Villa.

We nearly won the title in his first season under Graham Taylor and when Big Ron took over soon after we again finished as runner-up to Paul's old club United. He won the PFA Player of the Year award and won his first trophy with us in 1994, defeating Manchester United in the League Cup final, one of my best memories.

'God' eventually left Villa in '96, what a sad day being a youngster at the time, we sang a song to the tune of "Kumbayah" and we have a new one that we sing even now and always will out of respect. Macca retired in 1998, after short spells with Derby and Sheffield United.

<u>Personal View</u>

Paul remains my favourite player and I feel privileged to have watched him a lot. When I'm older and I can take my kids down the Villa and proudly say I saw him at his peak. The amazing thing with Paul was that he hardly trained, and some times on the pitch he was 'half soaked' but he always played well, he didn't make many mistakes and was very clever, his timing was immaculate, and he was great with his head, and scored the odd goal too. A proper Villa legend and always will be. Paul Mcgrath is in my heart forever.

IAN TAYLOR

Full name: Ian Kenneth Taylor
Date of birth: 4 June 1968
Place of birth: Birmingham, England
Playing position: Midfielder
Transfer Cost: £1M

Youth clubs
1991-1992 Moor Green

Senior clubs

Years	Club	App	Gls
1992-1994	Port Vale	83	28
1994	Sheffield Wednesday	14	1
1994-2003	Aston Villa	234	28
2003-2005	Derby County	81	14
2005-2007	Northampton Town	66	8
	Total	**478**	**79**

Ian became Brian Little's first signing in December 1994. He had spells with Moor Green, Port Vale and Sheffield Wednesday, Guy Whittingham moved as part of the deal.

He played, and scored, in the Villa side that won the 96 Coca-Cola cup final 3-0 against Leeds, whilst also netting a few goals in our 97/98 UEFA cup run, when we were knocked out to Atlético Madrid on away goals - remember Stan's goal?

A lifelong supporter of Villa, he used to stand in the Holte End as a kid and is often seen in the stands with the fans at away games, I have seen him a number of times at away games and I saw him at Good Hope Hospital when I went for a scan before my beautiful daughter was born. He was very happy to chat to the fans and always made the effort, combined with his committed displays and scoring crucial goals, he quickly became a favourite with the fans.

At derbies he is normally sitting amongst us claret and blue fans than living it up in the directors boxes, that makes him a true fan, he is one of us.

After leaving Villa in the summer of 2003, he ended up at Derby

County, where he was captain, and later Northampton Town.

Northampton Town and Ian announced on 23 April 2007 that the game against Huddersfield would be the last of his career. There were a lot of Villa fans who actually attended that game, out of great respect for the man and player.

He does a bit of commentating now that takes up some of his time and writes in the Villa match programmes.

It was announced on August 6th 2008 that Ian would be involved with Derby County for BBC Radio Derby during the 2008/09 season.

PERSONAL VIEW

Ian is a hero, a true great, a gentleman, a true Villa fan, he played his part in a lot of very important games for us, and he scored a lot. He loved scoring for us in front of the Holte End, he always made time for the fans that's why he is loved so much and always will be. Ian is a family man and its good to see he hardly misses a Villa game.

DEAN SAUNDERS

Full name: Dean Nicholas Saunders
Date of Birth: 21-6-1964
Place of birth: Swansea, Wales
Height: 5 ft 8 in
Playing position: Striker (past)
Transfer Cost: £2.3m

Current club
Wrexham (Manager)

Youth clubs
1980–1982   Swansea City

Senior clubs

Years	Club	App	Gls
1982–1985	Swansea City	49	12
1985	Cardiff City (loan)	4	0
1985–1987	Brighton & Hove Albion	72	21
1987–1988	Oxford United	59	22
1988–1991	Derby County	106	42
1991–1992	Liverpool	42	11
1992–1995	Aston Villa	110	37
1995–1996	Galatasaray	27	15
1996–1997	Nottingham Forest	43	5
1997–1998	Sheffield United	43	17
1998–1999	Benfica	17	5
1999–2001	Bradford City	44	3
	Total	**616**	**190**

National team
1986–2001   Wales   75   22

Teams managed
2008–   Wrexham

Deano scored two goals for Aston Villa in the League Cup final in 1994 against Manchester United, I will never forget that game growing up and seeing Villa at Wembley was a great occasion.

Dean Saunders was brought to Liverpool for £2.9 million from Derby by Graeme Souness just before the start of the 1991-92 season as a replacement for Peter Beardsley, and went on to become top scorer with 23 goals in 54 appearances as they won the FA Cup.

He became the first Liverpool player to score 4 goals in a European match. The Reds won the tie 6-1, 'Deano' also broke Roger Hunt's record for the most goals in one season, which was set way back in the 1964-65 season.

The following season Souness decided Deano wasn't needed and didn't feel he could play alongside Ian Rush so he sold him to the Villa, thanks very much Graeme, the best decision he ever made. His home debut for the Villa saw him score 2 against Liverpool when he ran their defence ragged! He also scored on his Anfield return for Villa that same season as we won 2-1.

After spells with Forest and Sheffield Utd, Deano rejoined Graeme at Benfica and again at Galatasary before moving to Bradford on a free at the start of the 1999-2000 season. So why did Souey sell him at Liverpool?

Personal View

What can you say about Deano, he was a fans' favourite, he was a great guy also and had time for the fans, he scored some screamers including hat-tricks, He formed a great partnership with Dalian Atkinson and was really popular amongst his team mates, he is a really nice helpful guy also, he rang me regarding the book while I was in Hamburg in December 2008 with the Villa. He is doing well now as manager of Wrexham.

PAUL MERSON

Full name: Paul Charles Merson
Date of birth: 20 March 1968
Place of birth: Harlesden, London,
Height: 5 ft 11
Playing position: Midfielder, Forward
Transfer Cost: £6.75M

SENIOR CLUBS

Years	Club	Apps	Gls
1985–1997	Arsenal	327	78
1987	Brentford (loan)	7	0
1997–1998	Middlesbrough	48	12
1998–2002	Aston Villa	117	18
2002–2003	Portsmouth	45	12
2003–2006	Walsall	77	6
2006	Tamworth	1	0
	Total	**622**	**126**

NATIONAL TEAM

1988–1990	England U21	4	0
1991–1998	England B	4	3
1991–1998	England	21	3

TEAMS MANAGED
2004–2006   Walsall

Magic Merse started his career at The Gunners, joining as an apprentice in 1984. He had a loan period at Brentford, he made his debut for Arsenal on November 22, 1986 against Man City, and he was a big part of George Graham's successful side at the end of the 80's. He was in the side that won the league on the last day of the season (remember Michael Thomas). He scored ten times that season and won the PFA Young Player of the Year.

He also won another League Title in 1991, the FA Cup and League Cup in '93, he scored in the League Cup final, and also won the Cup Winners' Cup in '94. He made his debut for England against Germany on September 11, 1991.

Paul helped The Gooners get to the Cup Winners' Cup final for the 2nd season in a row – they eventually lost to Spanish side Real Zaragoza, after Nayim scored a last minute goal from the half way line against a hapless David Seaman.

In 1997 Merson was sold to Boro for £4.5million which was a lot of money for a team in the division below the Premiership. He was a key player for their promotion as runners-up.

It was the autumn of 1998, that Merse was sold to us for £4million. He was with us for nearly five years, helping us reach the 2000 FA Cup final, he was given a free at the end of the 2001-02 season and he signed for Portsmouth, and was very important in the club's promotion to the big time in 2002-03.

He joined Walsall in the summer of 2003. Merson was eventually named manager following Colin Lee's sacking. He had a real hard job to try to keep Walsall in Division One. The month after relegation Merse was given the manager's job on a permanent contract.

2004-05 was difficult as Walsall went out of all the cups against lower league teams, and came close to another relegation.

After a difficult first season in management, he was sacked on 6 February 2006. Paul resumed his playing career at local team Tamworth, it only lasted for two before he retired on 9 March 2006.

Personal View

Paul is now often seen as a pundit on Soccer Saturday on Sky and he plays for Charity and also for the England Legends, he is a good pundit with a lot of knowledge but he does make a lot of people laugh also with his comments and style, he is a nice guy and I see him quite frequently around Sutton Coldfield. He was a magical signing for us at the time and I remember his debut well, he was so creative and we all remember his goal against Everton away, it was around the 30 yard mark when he lobbed the keeper, wonderful accuracy.

MARTIN LAURSEN

Full name: Martin Laursen
Date of birth: July 26, 1977
Place of birth: Fårvang, Denmark
Height: 6 ft 3 in (1.91 m)
Playing position: Centre Back
Nationality: Danish
Previous Clubs: AC Milan, Verona, Silkeborg IF
Position: Defender
Transfer Cost: £3M
Current Club: Retired

YOUTH CLUBS
Horn-Fårvang IF

SENIOR CLUBS

Years	Club	App	Gls
1995–1998	Silkeborg IF	35	1
1998–2001	Hellas Verona	58	3
2001	Parma	0	0
2001	A.C. Milan (loan)	22	2
2002–2004	A.C. Milan	10	0
2004–2009	Aston Villa	79	8

NATIONAL TEAM

2000 –	Denmark	53	2

Martin started his career with Danish Silkeborg IF, where he helped them secure second place in the 1997–98 season. He spent three seasons there before moving on to play for Serie B side Hellas Verona in Italy in August 98, and they managed to gain promotion to Serie A. He made his debut for Denmark in a friendly against Portugal in March 2000. He was a part of the squad in Euro 2000 although he didn't play a game due to injury.

Parma jointly owned Martin with Verona, and he made his move but was only there for three weeks of training at the club. He was chuffed to be picked up by A.C. Milan in a £8.7 million bid and began his career at the San Siro by scoring two goals in his first four matches.

On May 21, 2004, Villa signed him for £3 million, on a 4 year contract. Martin's debut was against Southampton, it was August 14, 2004, We won 2-0.

His time at Villa until recently was blighted by injury. He Played a few games during the 2004–05 season, but a recurring knee injury meant he played just one match for us during the 2005–06 season. He went to Bologna to try sort the injury out and he returned to the Villa team in August 2006. He managed to get over the problem and returned to form, and has been a massive part of O'Neill's plans. He is very relaxed and cool on the ball, and normally wins everything in the air. He is recognised as one of the best Premier League defenders around and scores his fair share of goals as well.

During the 2007–08 season, he scored 6 from defence, he played so well for us during the season and had a lot of man of the match awards.

He signed a new 2 and a half year deal with Villa on 17 January 2008 He was voted our Player of the Year in 2008 by the fans following his form in the whole season. In 2007-08 he played every single game for us in the league, it was a great personal achievement and he just grew and grew and gained a lot more confidence and made some outstanding performances.

Martin replaced Gareth Barry as captain for in the 2008-2009 season, and he is a great captain, a great leader and we wouldn't be the same team without him, we really missed him when he was out for a few months at the start of 2009. It was awful news though in the summer of 2009 when we heard that Martin was forced to retire through injury.

Personal View

Martin was really inspirational, a true leader, a true lion heart, the new Paul McGrath, It was a very sad day when he had to retire, it was just a shame he was injured so much at the start of his Villa career, he is so supportive of the young lads coming through and he gets involved in a lot of community work, he is a true gent and was a wonderful player.

ASHLEY YOUNG

Full name: Ashley Simon Young
Nationality: English
Date of Birth: 09/07/1985
Place of birth: Stevenage, England
Height: 5' 9"
Weight: 10st 3lbs
Country: England
Position: Midfielder
Transfer Cost: £9.75M

YOUTH CLUBS
2000–2002 Watford

SENIOR CLUBS
Years	Club	App	Gls
2002–2007	Watford	101	20
2007–	Aston Villa	105	21

NATIONAL TEAM
2006–2007	England U21	10	0
2007–	England	6	0

WATFORD

Young was 18 years old when he was handed his Watford début under Ray Lewington in September 2003, scoring as a sub against Millwall. He made five substitute appearances that season, scoring three goals, and had his first start for the club in the Worthington Cup. Young really excelled in the 2004-05 season, playing in 34 of the Hornets games as they just managed to survive in the Championship. His performance during that season earned him the club's Young Player of the Season award.

Aidy Boothroyd was the manager in the 2005–06 season, Ashley was given a new lease of life as a striker. He started 41 League matches, hitting the back of the net 15 times, as Watford qualified for the playoffs and beat Leeds 3–0 to achieve promotion back to the *Prem de le crem*.

In the January 2007 transfer window, there were teams who made

£5 million offers, Watford rejected any moves as well as an offer of £7 million, again from a club un-named. An offer of nearly £10 million from West Ham was accepted, but Young rejected the move, he wanted to wait for offers from clubs not involved in relegation.

Aston Villa

People were surprised when we paid what we did for Ashley, but I knew quite a bit about him and he always struck me as a real good tricky player going forward, the type Martin would go for.

On 31 January, Ashley went on to score on his debut for Villa at St James' Park against Newcastle United, but Villa went on to lose 3–1, a game I remember well.

He revelled in a free role just behind the front two, he had a lot of pace and invention making him a big threat to all defences. There was certainly an air of anticipation among Villa fans whenever he was in possession of the ball like Tony Daley in days gone by.

He missed only one match, at Fulham, when he was suspended after picking up five bookings, and scored nine goals, including 2 in the 5-1 victory v Birmingham City. Ashley had played for the England Under 21's and he made his full England debut as a second half sub against Austria in November 2007.

In the 2007–08 season, Young finished second to Cesc Fabregas in assists and also included in the Premier League Team of the Year. Ashley Young signed a new four-year contract until 2012 on the 4th November 2008.

Personal View

Ashley will always be a favourite 20 years down the line, he is the sort of player fans want to see, a player who takes on players who creates a lot for other players, who is always attack minded, he was an awesome signing definitely one of the best Villa players ever, and he can get better and better. I am sure he will represent England a lot more times in his career, he will be a really important player for our country, it would be great to see Ashley on the left and James Milner on the right, we have a lot of Villa players in the England team at present so let's see.

DWIGHT YORKE

Full name: Dwight Eversley Yorke
Date of birth: 3 November 1971
Place of birth: Canaan, Trinidad and Tobago
Height: 5 ft 9 in
Playing position: Midfielder, Striker
Transfer Cost: £120,000

SENIOR CLUBS

Years	Club	App	Gls
1989–1998	Aston Villa	232	73
1998–2002	Manchester United	95	47
2002–2004	Blackburn Rovers	60	12
2004–2005	Birmingham City	13	2
2005–2006	Sydney FC	21	7
2006– 2009	Sunderland	58	6
	Total	**479**	**147**

NATIONAL TEAM

1989– 2009	Trinidad and Tobago	72	19

Dwight has played for Sydney FC in the Australian A-League; and has previously played for Villa, Man Utd, Blackburn, and our rivals Birmingham, he was recently at Sunderland but has now retired. He left the international scene in 2001 after a difference of opinion with the manager, but he came back for the 2006 World Cup qualifiers.

Between 1989 and 1998, Yorke played for Villa. He was a winger until the 95-96 season, when he changed his role to centre-forward.

Dwight was discovered by Graham Taylor on a tour of the West Indies in 1989. Dwight was in a team that played a friendly against Villa, Graham was impressed and offered Dwight a trial at Villa, after which he was given a permanent contract and made his debut against Palace in 1990.

Yorke was a key player in the Villa team that reached the Coca Cola Cup Final in 1996. Villa beat Leeds 3-0 with Yorke getting the last goal of the three. In September 96, Dwight scored a hat-trick against Newcastle United in a 4-3 defeat. Newcastle were leading 3-1 and Villa were down to ten men, with Draper being sent off. Dwight was the last Villa player to score in front of the old Holte terrace, he scored both goals in a 2-1 win on the final day of the 1993-94 season, May 7th 1994, a game which I attended with my father.

Towards the end of Dwight's Villa career, he played in the game at Everton early in the season in August 98, but he hardly made any effort during the match as he was not happy at not being allowed to leave. Villa had no option but to sell him and he went to Man Utd for £12.6 million in Aug '98.

Dwight was a key player in helping the red devils to three successive Premier League titles including a well deserved treble of the Premier League title, F.A. Cup and Champions League.

In 2001-02, Dwight lost his place following Ruud van Nistelrooy's move to the club and the summer after he went to Blackburn for £2 million, spending two years there then he left to join Birmingham in a shock move in 2004 on a free. Dwight was eventually released from his contract not playing many games at all, and he signed for Sydney choosing to continue his career Down Under for less money than in other leagues, notably those in the Middle East which had bags of money. Dwight later had a spell at Sunderland.

Dwight spent 9 years at Villa he is not liked by some of our fans for his behaviour when he left us and also because he later went to the blues, stating they were a bigger club than us, but deep down I think we all still love Dwight, he was a great character around the place, and he was a real talent.

Personal View

Growing up watching Dwight was a delight, when you think of him, you can just see this massive smile, he loved his football, Birmingham was his second home, it was a lot for him to get used to. He was involved in a lot of very good games for us and real important games, he scored some crackers too, we were all very disappointed with his decision to leave, but I suppose deep down we thought we gave him his chance and he did play his heart our for us and United are a team with amazing history and tradition and were the best in England at the time. I don't think many would really begrudged him the chance to play for such a club.

GARETH BARRY

Date of Birth: 23/02/1981
Place of birth: Hastings
Height: 6' 0"
Weight: 12st 6lbs
Position: Midfielder
Transfer Cost: £50,000

Youth clubs
1996–1997   Brighton & Hove Albion

Senior clubs
Years	Club	App	Gls
1997– 2009	Aston Villa	441	52
2009–	Manchester City	16	1

National team
1998–2002	England U21	27	2
2007	England B	1	0
2000–	England	35	2

Gareth joined us from Brighton as a trainee in 1997 along with Michael Standing, who was at the time thought to be a much bigger talent than Barry. He played his first match for us on 2nd May 98 against Sheffield Wednesday. Initially, he played as a central defender, Gareth has become a very versatile player and captain. Starting as a centre-back in our defence to the left-back position. Later, Gareth settled into a left midfield role, but recently, he has switched to the centre of midfield.

As of April 2008, Barry was the longest serving player in the team. However in May 2008, Liverpool showed an interest in Gareth and offered up to £10 million which was rejected; they made more bids for Gareth, with a £13 million bid on 12 June 2008, also rejected, which was great news.

On 29 June 2008, Gareth, who still had 2 years left on his contract, criticised Martin O'Neill in a newspaper claiming no attempt had been made to keep him, He said: "Villa kept saying they wanted me to stay but I have not heard from the manager for weeks" and re-iterated his desire to join Liverpool to play in the Champions League.

Martin responded, stating that he and Randy gave the player numerous options and incentives to continue with the club. It led to Villa officially disciplining Barry on 2 July 2008 and another bid of £15 million from Liverpool was then also rejected as it was still short of our £18 million asking price. Finnan had been offered in a part-ex in the deal but the fee Villa wanted in this case was understood by the BBC to be £17 mill with Finnan.

On 31 July 2008 Villa announced that Gareth would be staying at Villa after an agreed deadline on a deal had passed, to be honest he was important to us but I just wanted an end to it all, but I'm glad he stayed for an extra season. Gareth scored for Villa as we beat Ajax 2-1 in our first Group F match of the UEFA Cup on 23 October 2008. after that a Premier League game at Wigan on 26th October 2008, he scored a penalty after Gabby was fouled in the area by Wigan's Bramble, we went on to win 4-0, I remember the coach trip home, we were bouncing all the way home, it completed a great week.

Personal View

A few seasons ago, I remembered thinking I couldn't imagine a Villa team without Gareth in it, he made us tick and was easily our best player. He was the engine, he was so accurate and positive and we played great passing football starting through Gareth, but when the transfer saga to Liverpool was going on I didn't really mind if he went. I like many fans just had enough of the uncertainty, but I was so happy he stayed and you cant argue his level of commitment in his last season.

In the summer of 2009, Gareth decided to move to Manchester City, this angered a lot of Aston Villa fans including me as Gareth said he wanted to move for Champions League Football and City weren't even in the Europa League... Everyone said he moved because of money and I suppose at the end of the day he was a great servant for us and not many of us would turn down trebling their wage, but if you were a Villa Fan then I'm sure we would of stayed loyal to the club and tried to push us into the Top 4.

STEVE STAUNTON

Date of birth: 19 January 1969
Place of birth: Drogheda, Republic of Ireland
Height: 6 ft 1
Playing position: Defender
Transfer Cost: £1.1M

SENIOR CLUBS

Years	Club	App	Gls
1985–1986	Dundalk		
1986–1991	Liverpool	65	0
1987	Bradford C (loan)	8	0
1991–1998	Aston Villa	205	16
1998–2000	Liverpool	44	0
2000	Crystal P (loan)	6	1
2000–2003	Aston Villa	73	0
2003–2005	Coventry City	70	4
2005–2006	Walsall	7	0
	Total	**478**	**21**

NATIONAL TEAM

1987–1989	Republic of Ireland U21	4	0
1988–2002	Republic of Ireland	102	8

TEAMS MANAGED

2006–2007	Republic of Ireland
2009-	Darlington

Steve was scouted by Liverpool when he was at Dundalk as a 17 year old and was signed on the 2 September 1986 by Kenny Dalglish. He eventually made his debut on 17 September 1988 in a 1–1 draw against Spurs. He scored his first goal on 20 September against Arsenal. His career at Liverpool went from strength to strength although he was never a first team regular.

He joined us on 7th August 1991 for £1.1m and he made a great start on his début on the 17th August when he scored in the 3–2 win over Sheffield Wednesday Away. He became a regular in our defence as we finished 7th during the 1991–92 season. He was a key player when we finished 2nd in the first Premier League season. We will get there again, keep the faith!!!

The season after Steve won a Coca-Cola League Cup winners medal when he helped us by beat United 3–1 at Wembley. In 1994/95 he had a good season and captained us also. The 1995–96 season was not a great one for 'Stan' as he was injured a lot but he did get a medal in the League cup final against Leeds even though he didn't come off the bench.

During the 1996-1998 seasons he was again a very big important player for us, then his contract was about to expire and he had a move back to Merseyside with the Reds on 3 July 1998 on a Bosman.

His 2nd stint at Anfield didn't last too long and on 7th December 2000 he came back to Villa park on a free, after Stan left us the 2nd time he continued to play with Coventry City, he went there on 15 August 2003 on yes you guessed it a Free transfer. He played quite a few times there and instead of renewing his stay at Coventry he ended up at Walsall on 2 August 2005. He didn't play that many times there before he was appointed manager of the Republic of Ireland, a reign that ended with failure to qualify for the 2008 European Championships.

On 4 February 2008, Stan joined Leeds United as Gary McAllister's assistant at the club. When Gary was sacked by Leeds in December 2008 after five defeats in a row, Stan also left the club.

Personal View

What a left foot, his goal against Man Utd at Old Trafford stands out - a rocket which swerved past Schmeichel into the keeper's left top corner. He scored some screamers and was always very well organised, a great player and a proper professional. I was surprised when he went into management though, I think he would of done better with Macca and Houghton as his Number 2's...

DION DUBLIN

Position: Forward
Place of Birth: Leicester
Date Of Birth: 22/ 04/ 1969
Height: 6'2
Weight: 12st 4lbs
Transfer Cost: £5.75m

SENIOR CLUBS

YEARS	CLUB	APP	GLS
1988	Norwich City	0	0
1988–1992	Cambridge United	156	52
1988	Barnet (loan)	1	0
1992–1994	Manchester United	12	2
1994–1998	Coventry City	145	61
1998–2004	Aston Villa	155	48
2002	Millwall (loan)	5	2
2004–2006	Leicester City	58	5
2006	Celtic	11	1
2006–2008	Norwich City	70	12
	Total	613	183

NATIONAL TEAM
1998	England	4	0

Dion began his career with Norwich in 1985, but he never made the first team and was given a free in 1988. He signed for Cambridge and his goalscoring exploits won them promotion from the Fourth to Second Division in successive seasons. In 1991-92, he was a big part in helping them finish in a club-best 5th place in the last season of the old Second Division, but when they failed to win promotion via the playoffs Dion was put up for sale. He was sold to Man United for £1m, but missed a lot of the 1992-93 season following a broken leg just a few games into his Old Trafford career - he did have enough league appearances though for a Premiership winners medal.

In 93-94, he regained his fitness but his team chances were restricted. Dion's long-term injury had forced Alex Ferguson to seek a new forward and the arrival of Eric Cantona ended Dion's chances. He was left out of the FA Cup winners team and failed to get enough apps for another Premier title medal, and was sold to Coventry for £2m.

In four-and-a-half years with Coventry, Dion established himself as one of the Premiership's top strikers, He equalled the Coventry City record for most goals in a top flight season with 23 (18 League, 4 FA Cup, 1 Coca Cola Cup).

In 1998 he was sold to Villa for £4.5m. The following season he helped us get to our first FA Cup final in 43 years, despite missing a lot of the season with a broken neck! Whilst playing for Villa against Sheffield Wednesday he had the life threatening injury and as a result he now has a titanium plate holding 3 neck vertebrae together.

In March 2002 he signed on loan with Millwall which would keep him at the Den for the rest of the season, He helped them reach the First Division play offs and returned to Villa at the end of the season, with his future in doubt.

In 2002/03 Dion worked harder than ever and got back into the first eleven. Finishing top goal scorer with a total of 15, Dublin's season was only marred by the Midlands Derby game against Blues in March. He got a red card for violent conduct when he nutted Savage - a great moment as someone was bound to nut him sooner or later! Dion said his behaviour was provoked by racist remarks, but he eventually apologised.

Dublin remained on the Villa payroll until his contract expired in the summer of 2004 and he was given a free. He was signed by Leicester, who was then in the championship. In the Jan 06 transfer window Celtic became Dion's 8th club when he joined them on a free in a move that initially fans were thinking what the hell are we doing with a 37 year old. They soon got to like Dion when he went on to score in the 3-0 League Cup Final victory against Dunfermline, and his place in Celtic hearts was confirmed.

Personal View

Dion will never be forgotten for nutting Savage, that's my best memory of Dion, I do remember when we signed him, it was a great signing and he scored loads for us when he first joined including a hat-trick at Southampton. I remember watching him away at Highfield Road also and he scored against Coventry on his return, that was a great moment, and he scored at Home against Arsenal when we were 2-0 down and won 3-2, what a game that was! He is a funny guy but very clever he does a lot of work with Sky now commentating and it is always interesting to hear his views.

THOMAS HITZLSPERGER

Date of birth: 5 April 1982
Place of birth: Munich, West Germany
Height: 6ft
Playing position: Left midfielder, Central midfielder
Transfer Cost: FREE

YOUTH CLUBS
1989	VFB Forstinning
1989–2000	Bayern Munich
2000–2001	Aston Villa

SENIOR CLUBS
Years	Club	App	Gls
2001–2005	Aston Villa	99	8
2001–2002	Chesterfield (loan)	5	0
2005–2010	VfB Stuttgart	126	20
2010-	Lazio		

NATIONAL TEAM
Years	Team	App	Gls
2002–2004	Germany U-21	20	3
2004–	Germany	51	6

Tommy joined us in August 2000 on a free from Bayern Munich. He had had a trial with Celtic after leaving Bayern but he fancied a move to the Midlands instead of Scotland.

His first game was the 3–0 home defeat by Liverpool in January 2001, that was his only game that season. He was loaned out to Chesterfield during the 2001–02 season, and he made his first appearance against Kidderminster in the LDV Vans Trophy. He scored 6 first team goals for the Kiddies. He was recalled by Villa during the 2nd month of the loan spell however, as we had a lot of players injured or suspended. Tommy made more of a Villa breakthrough following the arrival of Graham Taylor and a lot of games under David O'Leary. He left us on good terms, I think we all missed his funny accent, a mixture of Brummie and German! - and he said that he would return if the opportunity arose, lets hope so because it seems he has really improved himself. His nickname at the Villa was 'der Hammer' because of his left-foot shot, he had a real powerful shot from long-range. Tommy signed for Stuttgart in 2005, leaving us on a Free. He won the Bundesliga title in his 2nd season and on 14 August 2007, he had a contract extension until the summer of 2010, after which he will hopefully re-sign for us. Since July 2008 Tommy has been made captain.

Personal View

He was a proper player, he moved well, passed well, shot well, he was never scared to shoot anywhere outside the box he had the ability and the power to do it, everyone loved the sort of player tommy was, it was a shame he left us especially at the time he did, we shouldn't of let a player like him go. He has done really well though since leaving including playing a lot for Germany, he is a very important player for club and country.

SHAUN TEALE

Date of birth: March 10, 1964
Place of birth: Southport
Height: 6 ft
Playing position: Defender
Transfer Cost: £300,000

SENIOR CLUBS

Years	Club	App	Gls
1988-1989	Weymouth		
1989-1991	Bournemouth	100	4
1991-1995	Aston Villa	147	2
1995-1998	Tranmere Rovers	54	0
1997	Preston North End (loan)	5	0
1997-1998	Sing Tao		
1998-2000	Motherwell	47	4
2000	Carlisle United	18	0
2000-2002	Southport	68	5
2002-2003	Burscough		
2003-2004	Northwich Victoria	6	1
	Total	445	16

TEAMS MANAGED

2002-2003 Burscough
2003-2004 Northwich Victoria
2005-2006 Chorley

Shaun was a great professional who played in the centre of defence, he joined Bournemouth from Weymouth for £50k in 1989. He was at Bournemouth before his big move to the Villa. The thing that most stands out to me of Shaun when I was a kid was the magical Coca Cola Cup semi finals against Tranmere Rovers. He formed a rock solid partnership with Macca. Upon leaving Villa he had a spell with Tranmere Rovers and was a rock in the centre of defence for Motherwell in the Scottish Prem. He then went on to join Southport before moving into coaching and management in the non league.

Shaun was named manager of Burscough, who were in the Unibond Premier Division. Whilst he was there, they won the 2003 FA Trophy, a great achievement.

Shaun did leave Burscough six weeks later and has since managed Northwich Victoria, a Conference team in the 2003/04 season. He left Northwich after the 2003/04 season.

Between February 2005 and August 2006, he managed Northern Premier League First Division side Chorley, before leaving and now he runs his own successful pub and restaurant business in Burscough.

<u>Personal View</u>

Shaun was a rock with Macca, they made it look so easy both really loved going in hard and rarely missed a tackle, the games against Tranmere were great including his goal in the 2nd leg at Villa Park which helped us get to the final. When I look back on my childhood supporting Villa, the players that mainly stay in my mind are Shaun, Macca, Deano, Daley, Froggatt and he will always be remembered as a good professional and a very clever and tough defender.

DALIAN ATKINSON

Date of birth: March 21, 1968
Place of birth: Shrewsbury, England
Height: 6 ft 0 in (1.83 m)
Playing position: Striker
Transfer Cost: £1.6m

Senior clubs

Years	Club	App	Gls
1985–1989	Ipswich Town	60	18
1989–1990	Sheffield Wed	38	10
1990–1991	Real Sociedad	26	12
1991–1995	Aston Villa	85	23
1995–1996	Fenerbahce S.k	21	10
1996	Metz (Loan)		
1996–1997	Manchester City	8	2
1998–1999	Al-ittihad		
2001	Daejeon Citizen (Loan)	3	1
2001	Jeonbuk Hyundai Motors	5	0
	Total	246	76

National team

1990	England B	1	1

Dalian is mainly remembered for his magnificent solo effort against Wimbledon. He is also remembered by Villa fans for his wonderful performance and goal in the 94 Coca-Cola Cup final win against United. Atkinson was at Ipswich Town as a youngster, impressing all with his speed and shooting range. He then moved on to Sheffield Wednesday.

When signed by the Villa, he former a lethal partnership alongside Deano, when the Welshman arrived from Liverpool. The deadly duo's partnership came to an end in 1995 when the players were both sold to Turkish clubs - Deano to Galatasaray and Dalian to Fenerbahçe, I was gutted at the time. 'Dales' failed to settle in Turkey and had loans with FC Metz and Man City before leaving in 1997 and finishing his career with teams in Saudi Arabia and South Korea.

Personal View

You cant imagine Dalian playing without Deano, they were such a great exciting partnership and really implemented each other well, they scored some amazing goals for us, real important goals, it's a shame he wasn't there longer to be honest. I remember being at the back of the Holte End when Dalian scored against Man Utd, but Lee Sharpe won the game for the Red Devils, it was mad back then being a young lad, it really hurt losing a game especially against the big boys. We had a wonderful squad, it was a great era capped off with the cup final against United where the deadly duo both scored.

NOLBERTO SOLANO

Date of birth: December 12, 1974
Place of birth: Callao, Peru
Height: 5 ft 9
Playing position: Midfielder
Transfer Cost: £1.5M

Youth clubs
1986-1992   Sporting Cristal

Senior clubs

Years	Club	App	Gls
1992-1993	Sporting Cristal	0	0
1993-1994	Deportivo Municipal	24	2
1994-1997	Sporting Cristal	77	31
1997-1998	Boca Juniors	32	5
1998-2004	Newcastle United	172	29
2004-2005	Aston Villa	49	8
2005-2007	Newcastle United	58	8
2007-2008	West Ham United	23	4
2008-2009	Larissa	17	2
2009-2010	Univ. de Deportes	32	10
2010-	Leicester City		

National team

1994-	Peru	95	20

Nobby spent much of his career in the best league in the world, the Premier League. He is a massively popular in Peru, he is easily one of the most recognisable names in Peru and will always be thought of fondly. In fact he is that well known in his native country that he has a postage stamp with his name and picture on it.

Nobby is the first Peruvian to play in the Premiership, In 1998 he signed a contract with Newcastle for £2.4m. His debut came in a match against Chelsea which was on August 22. In June 2001, Nobby had signed a new contract which meant he was staying at Newcastle for another five years, but eventually he was sold to us in 2004, the Newcastle fans were fuming as Nobby was easily one of their best players.

Nobby joined in January 2004 for a fee of £1.5m and signed a two-and-a-half year contract. He first game was a 5-0 win over Leicester City, I was there it was a great result, it was the game when a Leicester season ticket holder came onto the pitch to have a go at the then Leicester keeper Ian Walker. Nobby became our Player of the Year later on.

Solano returned to the Geordies in August 2005 for £1.5 million with Milner coming to us on a season-long loan. Nobby then signed for West Ham in August 2007. His first goal for The Hammers was a typical free-kick in a 5-0 away win against Derby on in November 2007. He was released by them in 2008.

Personal View

Nobby was such a exciting player to watch, he really made you sit up and pay attention whenever he was on the ball, he is the sort of player you would pay to watch, he scored some great goals for villa, important goals, he added so much needed skill and flair to our team.

TONY DALEY

Full name: Anthony Mark Daley
Date of birth: October 18, 1967
Place of birth: Birmingham, England
Height: 5 ft 8
Playing position: Winger

CURRENT CLUB
Wolverhampton Wanderers (fitness coach)

SENIOR CLUBS

Years	Club	App	Gls
1985-1994	Aston Villa	233	31
1994-1998	Wolverhampton Wanderers	21	3
1998-1999	Watford	12	1
1999	Walsall	7	0
1999-2002	Forest Green Rovers	67	6
	Total	340	41

NATIONAL TEAM

1990	England B	1	0
1991-1992	England	7	0

Tony signed for the Villa as an apprentice and made his debut when he was 17 on April 20, 1985 in a 2-0 defeat at Southampton. He played for us for 10 seasons, and finished a runner-up in the 1989/90 and 1992/93 seasons. He also played in our great day at Wembley in 1994 in the Coca Cola Cup final against Manchester United.

Tony played a total of 7 times for England between 1991 and 1992 under Taylor. His full debut was as a sub in Poland on November 13, 1991 that saw us qualify for the 1992 European Championships in Sweden. He was chosen for the squad and played his part in 2 of England's 3 games there, but after that he was never selected again, what a waste of his talent.

Daley joined Taylor again as he left us for local rivals Wolves in July 94 for £1.25 million, but he had a lot of injuries and he only played 21 games for the club in 4 seasons.

He was signed again by yes you guessed it Graham Taylor at Watford in July 1998 on a free. His injuries recurred though and he missed the final few months as they got promoted to the Premiership. He eventually left for Walsall in June 1999, before playing for Forest Green, hanging up his boots in 2002.

When he finished his playing career, he did a Bachelor of Science degree in Sports and Exercise Science and stayed at Forest Green as a fitness coach and worked with the youth players at Villa's Academy.

He then joined Sheffield United as a Fitness and Conditioning Coach in 2003 but he eventually quit following a difference of opinion with Bryan Robson on August 30, 2007. He then joined the Wolves in the same position.

Personal View

I saw a lot of Tony as a young boy and he was so dazzling, so exciting to watch, the wing–wizard, it was a shame he had so many injuries as he should of played for England a lot more than he did, he is a very helpful pleasant guy and he is still loving being involved in football.

UGO EHIOGU

Full name: Ugochuku Ehiogu
Date of birth: 3 November 1972
Place of birth: London
Height: 6 ft 3
Playing position: Centre Back
Transfer Cost: £40,000

Senior clubs

Years	Club	App	Gls
1989–1991	WBA	2	0
1991–2000	Aston Villa	237	12
2000–2007	Middlesbrough	126	7
2006–2007	Leeds United (Loan)	6	1
2007–2008	Rangers	9	1
2008–2009	Sheffield United	26	1

National team

Years	Team	App	Gls
1992–1993	England U21	15	1
1994	England B	1	0
1996–2002	England	4	1

Ugo started his career at West Brom before Big Ron brought him to Villa for £40,000 in August 91. By 1994, he replaced one of my favourites Shaun Teale as the main partner to Macca. He was great at the Villa and he played in over 300 games for us. He was in the team that beat Leeds 3–0 in the 1996 cup final. He joined Boro from Villa in November 2000 for a total of £8 million. Ugo became a massive player for them and he rejoined Southgate in the defence.

On 23 November 2006 he moved to Elland Road to join Leeds United on loan for two months. He scored one goal in his time at Leeds.

He was eventually released from the Boro and on 22nd January, 2007, he signed a contract with Rangers for 18 months. His first goal was not one he was known for scoring normally with his head but with an overhead kick in his first game against the deadly rivals Celtic, giving Rangers a 1–0 win. He eventually won Goal of the season for that goal.

On 16 January 2008, he signed for Sheffield United and his first game was in a 1–1 draw with Watford and he played a lot in the team that season.

Personal View

Everyone loved Ugo, it was just his presence in the defence, a big powerful centre back who came up with the odd goal. He was also a great defender, you can never forget his name, it's a shame he didn't play for England that much and he was struck with a lot of injuries, but he was a good player who always gave his best and played in a lot of memorable games for us.

OLOF MELLBERG

Full name: Erik Olof Mellberg
Date of birth: September 3, 1977
Place of birth: Gullspång, Sweden
Height: 6 ft 1
Playing position: Centre back
Transfer Cost: £5M

SENIOR CLUBS

Years	Club	App	Gls
1996–1997	Degafors	47	0
1997–1998	AIK	17	0
1998–2001	Racing Santander	17	0
2001–2008	Aston Villa	232	8
2008–2009	Juventus	27	2
2009	Olympiakos	10	1

NATIONAL TEAM

2000–	Sweden	98	7

Olof the great started at Swedish team Degerfors IF and when they were relegated Olof went to AIK, before being he was sold after 10 months in the side. Racing Santander came in for him and he made the move to Spain where he was outstanding for the team.

Villa were lucky to get Olof at the time as Barcelona and Valencia were both in for him, but he decided to come to us and quite soon he was made the captain for a long time.

In 2007 O'Neill made Olof his Number 1 choice in defence and on the opening day of the 2006–07 League season he became the first scorer at Arsenal's new Emirates Stadium. In the 2007–08 season, he played right back after we purchased Zat Knight.

January 2008 was a sad time for the Villa fans when it was announced that Olof had signed a pre-contract agreement with Juventus. In his final game for Villa at Upton Park, he gave every fan that attended a home or an away shirt which said Thanks 4 Your Support. What a great generous gesture.

Personal View

Olof was a massive player for us, no one had really heard of him before he came, but he played his heart out for us even when he was out of his favoured position, he played well with whoever was put alongside him, he scored the odd goal and loved the fans. He will never be forgotten by the fans, we wish him all the best for the future.

GABRIEL AGBONLAHOR

Full name Gabriel Imuetinyan Agbonlahor
Nationality: English
Date of Birth: 13/10/1986
Place of birth : Birmingham, England
Height: 5' 11"
Weight: 12st 5lbs
Previous Clubs: Sheffield Wed (loan), Watford (loan)
Position: Striker
Squad Number: 11

YOUTH CLUBS
1994–2005 Aston Villa

SENIOR CLUBS
Years	Club	App	Gls
2005–	Aston Villa	140	40
2005	Watford (loan)	2	0
2005	Sheffield Wednesday (loan)	8	0

NATIONAL TEAM
2006–2008	England U21	16	5
2008–	England	3	0

Gabby was first noticed playing for local side Great Barr Falcons, where his pace brought him success as a young teenager. In the 2002–03 season, playing his first season for the Villa Academy, he notched 9 goals in 18 appearances. He then finished with a tally of 35 goals in 29 games in the 2003–04 season, a feat which was compared to Vassell's 38 goals in the 1997–98 season. Gabby showed a lot of promise in the Youth setup, he made more of an impact for the Reserves in the 2004–05 season, where he scored 18 goals in 22 games to bring his youth total to 71 appearances and 62 goals.

Gabby made 37 apps for the reserves between 2003 and 2006, and scored 19 times, most notably a hat-trick against Tim Howard in a 3–0 defeat of Man United Reserves. He also captained an Aston Villa team in the 2006 HKFC Philips Lighting International Soccer Sevens, and with that he was named "Player of the Tournament" as Villa finished Runners-Up to Urawa Red Diamonds.

His first taste of proper first team football came in October 2005 when he went on loan to Sheffield Wednesday for 2 months.

Aston Villa 2005–06 season

Gabby made his Premiership debut on 18 March, 2006, against Everton Away, He scored on his debut after 63 minutes, although we went on to lose 4–1. I remember the game well, he was so fast and I remember looking through the Villa programme and he scored so many in the reserves lists in there so we all felt he could be massive for us.

2006–07 season

In the pre-season games before the 2006–07 season, Gabby netted four goals in five games for us including two against Walsall.

Gabby started on the right wing in O'Neill's new look side, and was part of the team that managed a get a point from the first ever game at Arsenal's new Emirates Stadium. Gabby's first goal of the season came at home against Charlton, in a 2–0 win. On 30 September, he scored a crucial equaliser against Premier champions Chelsea heading in Ridgewell's cross with a header to earn Villa a hard-earned well deserved 1–1 draw.

Gabby scored an extra-time injury-time winner to beat Leicester at the Walkers Stadium 3-2. Gabby scored a lot against the big teams when Manchester United were added to a list of his victims that also included Chelsea and Liverpool.

2007–08 season

Gabby scored the vital second goal in the match between Aston Villa and Chelsea on 2 September, which Villa won 2–0, I remember it well it was a cross from Ashley Young. Gabby scored the winner in the 86th minute of the Birmingham Derby, that was the best feeling I had for a long time, it was 60 seconds after saving the ball on the line from Ridgewell's shot. After 13 games, Gabby was our top goal scorer, with 6 League goals. On 7 December Agbonlahor won the League's Player of the month award and Manager O'Neill won Manager of the month award.

2008–09 SEASON

On 15 August 2008, Agbonlahor signed a new 4-year deal, tying him to us until 2012. Following his contract extension, on 17 August, 2008, the opening game of the new season, he scored a hat-trick against Man City. All three goals were scored in the space of 7 amazing minutes, it was the 2nd fastest hat-trick in the history of the League. He was named man of the match in a 4-2 victory, what a start!!

Gabby ended as our top scorer but sadly it wasn't enough to earn a top 4 finish. The 2009/10 season has continued in a similar vein for the lad, a winner at Old Trafford being one particular highlight.

PERSONAL VIEW

Gabby is electric, he can be really good with his feet too but sometimes he doesn't seem to read the game as he should, and a lot of villa fans including myself moan that all he has is pace. He is a good finisher sometimes but a lot of the time he seems lazy, it might be unfair as he is still young and still learning. He has been important so far in this season and has broken into the England team, he could become so much better though if he makes a bit more effort in some games.

THE VILLA PREMIER YEARS - 1992-2010

MARK BOSNICH

Full name: Mark Bosnich
Date of birth: 13 January 1972
Place of birth: Fairfield, Australia
Height: 6ft 1
Playing position: Goalkeeper
Current Club: Sydney Olympic
Transfer Cost: FREE

YOUTH CLUBS
1988–1989   Sydney Croatia

SENIOR CLUBS

Years	Club	App	Gls
1988–1989	Sydney Croatia	5	0
1989–1992	Manchester United	3	0
1992–1999	Aston Villa	179	0
1999–2001	Manchester United	23	0
2001–2003	Chelsea	5	0
2008	Central Coast Mariners	4	0
2009 -	Sydney Olympic	7	0

NATIONAL TEAM
1993–2000   Australia   17   1

In 1988, at the age of 16, Mark moved to England to join Man Utd and made his debut against Wimbledon in the First Division on 30 April 1990. He only ended playing two more games for the club and signed for the Villa on a free in Feb 92. During his time at United, he won the FA Cup and the Cup Winners' Cup but he failed to make the Team for both.

Mark didn't have a regular place in the Villa team until the 93-94 season. He was a hero against Tranmere Rovers that season, he brilliantly stopped three shots in a dramatic penalty shootout, I remember that so well, it was a wonderful feeling knowing we were on the way to Wembley. We went on to win the final against Manchester United.

In 1994-95 It was his first full season as our first-choice, but it wasn't the greatest season for us. 1995-96 was the best season of Mark's career as he helped us finish 4th and win the Coca Cola Cup final at Wembley with a 3-0 win over Leeds.

He spent three more seasons at Villa before he joined Man United on a free in 1999 as successor to Peter Schmeichel who went the other way but he played infrequently for United and moved to Chelsea in 2001. In September 2002 he failed a drugs test and was sacked by Chelsea and banned for nine months, that was probably his worst moment in football.

Mark has been out of football for a while but he played for Central Coast Mariners in a pre-season cup game against Sydney on July 27, 2008. He kept a clean sheet and played very well including saving a penalty. On Tuesday 19th August 2008 Mark signed a 7 week deal. Mark had his A-League debut with the Central Coast Mariners in August 2008 in a 2–4 away win against the Queensland Roar in Brisbane.

Personal View

Mark was a hero against Tranmere Rovers in the League cup semi final 1994, from that moment onwards he really stood out, he made so many amazing reflex saves, he was an awesome shot stopper and worked really hard in training. We have had some great goalkeepers down the years and Mark really was one of the best.

GARETH SOUTHGATE

Date of birth: 3 September 1970
Place of birth: Watford
Height: 6 ft
Playing position: Centre Back
Transfer Cost: £2.5M

Senior clubs

Years	Club		App	Gls
1988–1995	Crystal Palace		152	15
1995–2001	Aston Villa		192	7
2001–2006	Middlesbrough		160	4
		Total	504	26

National team

1995–2004	England	57	2

Teams managed

2006–2009 Middlesbrough

Gareth began his career at Crystal Palace, playing in midfield. He became captain and helped them lift the 1994 Division One title. After they were relegated he moved to Villa.

Gareth joined us in July '95, He was moved to centre-back by manager Brian Little, and he became a great defender for club and country. He made his England debut in 1996. In Euro '96 Southgate played a important role in England's Run. Unfortunately Gareth missed the penalty that sent us out. He carried on playing well after for Villa getting the captain's armband, and he was a great captain for us.

Gareth played every game during the 1998/99 season. He slipped out of the England team at this time but became the backbone of our defence during Ugo's absence from the team and guided Our Barry through his early stages at the top level.

Gareth had another great season in 1999/00, but he handed in a transfer request just before Euro 2000. Gregory rejected all offers for his captain, and was determined to keep him at Villa. Southgate did though eventually leave us though to sign for Middlesbrough.

Later he turned to management with Middlesbrough when he replaced Steve McClaren in June 2006. The appointment had been in question by the LMA as he did not hold a UEFA Pro-Licence. However chairman Steve Gibson believes he has the right man for the job, saying "No-one knows this club like Gareth does and I do". Gareth left Middlesbrough in 2009.

Personal View

He always gave his all for the Villa, it was just a shame he left for a club like Middlesbrough you could of understood at the time if he went to Man Utd or Arsenal but Middlesbrough I don't know what he was thinking... However he stayed there for some time was an honest manager and it was good to see an English manager get the chance in the Premier League, as there are too many foreign managers and players in the game. I am sure he will return to management some day.

GORDON COWANS

Full name Gordon Sidney Cowans
Date of birth October 27, 1958
Place of birth West Cornforth, County Durham
Height 5 ft 7
Playing position Midfielder

SENIOR CLUBS

Years	Club	App	Gls
1976–1985	Aston Villa	286	42
1985–1988	A.S Bari	94	3
1988–1991	Aston Villa	117	7
1991–1993	Blackburn Rovers	50	2
1993–1994	Aston Villa	11	0
1994	Derby County	36	0
1994–1995	Wolverhampton W.	37	0
1995–1996	Sheffield United	21	0
1996–1997	Bradford City	25	0
1997	Stockport County	7	0
1997	Burnley	6	0

NATIONAL TEAM

1980 -1990	England B	2	0
1983 -1990	England	10	2

Sid began at Villa in 1974, which was the start of something special and he signed in 1976. At the mighty Villa he won the League Cup, a Championship, European Cup and the European Super Cup.

He left us in 1985 for Bari. He came back to us in 1988 but left again in 1991 when he went to Ewood Park and played for Blackburn then he came back to us, before moving to Derby, Wolves, Sheff Utd, Bradford, Stockport and lastly Burnley. He played for the three lions 10 times and he scored two goals. Sid is back at Villa once more Aston Villa as a coach and looks after the highly successful youth academy.

Personal View

I didn't really see much of Gordon in his early career as I was born after the European Cup win in 1982, I have met him a number of times since however and he always takes the time to talk to the fans and have his picture taken. A true gentleman he loves interacting with the fans and is always very pleasant. As I grew up I was aware how popular and important he was to the club and the fans, and footage I have seen of him was awesome, I saw him play a few times in the early 90's and I have followed him a lot in the Villa Old Stars team and it is clear he still has 'it'. It's great to see him still involved with the club and I wish we could get a lot more former players back involved.

PHILIP GEOFFREY KING

Date of birth: December 28, 1967
Place of birth: Bristol, England
Height: 5 ft 8 in
Playing position: Defender

SENIOR CLUBS

Years	Club	App	Gls
1985-1986	Exeter City	27	0
1986-1987	Torquay United	24	3
1987-1989	Swindon Town	116	4
1989-1994	Sheffield Wednesday	129	2
1993	Notts County	6	0
1994-1997	Aston Villa	4	0
1995	WBA	5	0
1997-1999	Swindon Town	6	0
1997	Blackpool	16	0
1999	Brighton & Hove Alb.	3	0
1999-2000	Kidderminster H.	14	2
2000-2001	Bath City	0	0
2004	Cinderford Town	1	0

Phil joined Big Ron at Villa for a fee of £250k in August 1994, he had previously played under Ron at Sheffield Wednesday. He started his career at the Villa very well - scoring the winning penalty in the UEFA Cup against the mighty Inter Milan. I remember that game well as I was so nervous in the stadium, it came down to one kick of the ball and he scored and he just stood there with his arms in the air and the whole stadium was rocking. Brian Little was our new Manager and Phil was unlucky that he didn't get to play much and moved further out of the reckoning after we signed little Alan Wright from Blackburn.

He left for the Baggies on loan in October 95 and was injured for a while and he returned to fitness and played a lot in our reserve side until leaving in March 1997 to go to Swindon Town where he had been previously in his career on a free and further down the line he had another loan spell at Blackpool until he had another free to Brighton in March 99. He played 3 times for the seagulls.

He left for Chester City and later on he decided to join Kidderminster Harriers in August 99. He won the League Title there the season after, further down the line he moved to Bath City on a free in July 2000.

In March 2004, King played for Cinderford Town as a favour to a friend. Phil is now retired but he plays for the Villa in the Masters Football Tournament and he is still involved with Swindon Town. He also does some commentary on Swindon Town matches for Radio Wiltshire.

Personal View

Phil was unlucky with injuries so it was a shame he didn't play that much for us and Brian Little didn't give him much of a chance when he became manager, but Phil was a good professional and always gave his all for us, he is a very nice helpful guy who has helped me with doing a review for this book and meeting me to sign a few copies.

JAMES MILNER

Date of birth: 4 January 1986 (age 24)
Place of birth: Wortley, Leeds,
Height: 5 ft 9 in
Playing position: Winger

Youth career
1996–2002 Leeds United

Senior career

Years	Club	App	Goals
2002–2004	Leeds United	54	5
2003	Swindon Town (loan)	6	2
2004–2008	Newcastle United	94	8
2005–2006	Aston Villa (loan)	33	3
2008 -	Aston Villa	55	7

National team

2004–2009	England U21	46	9
2009–	England	6	0

Leeds United

Milner's debut for Leeds came on the 10th November 2002, in a game against the Hammers, when he came on as a substitute for Jason Wilcox for the last 6 minutes. The appearance made him the 2nd youngest player ever to play in the Prem, at the age of 16 years and 309 days. On Boxing Day of the same year, he became the youngest ever player to score in the Prem, with a goal in a 2–1 win vs Sunderland. The record is now owned by James Vaughan of Everton. James then moved on to the North East to play for Newcastle United, then he made a successful loan move to the mighty Villains.

Loan Move to Aston Villa

James made his debut for us on the 12th September 2005 in a Prem match against the Hammers. 5 days later, he scored his 1st goal in a 1–1 draw against the Spurs. In a League Cup game in the same week, James helped us from being 3–1 down at half-time to win 8–3 against Wycombe, he scored 2 goals in the 2nd half fightback.

James said that he would like to join Villa permanently because of the opportunity of more regular starts. O'Leary confirmed during the season that he would like James to join us permanently, but doubted he would be given the opportunity to sign him. Shortly before the end of his loan period, negotiations between Villa and Newcastle began.

The newly-appointed Newcastle manager Glenn Roeder expressed a desire that James remain a Newcastle player. This, as well as the departure of O'Leary and the shortage of money at Villa, meant that a deal to sign James permanently seemed unlikely. In June, it became even less likely when we rejected an offer of James as part of a trade for Barry. However, the deal was resurrected when the best day ever happened and we were taken over by American billionaire Randy Lerner, and O'Neill was appointed as our new manager. We made an improved offer on 30 August, which was accepted by Newcastle. Media sources quoted the transfer as being £4m. A move appeared to have been agreed, but at the last moment Newcastle recalled James and talks broke down.

RETURN TO NEWCASTLE UNITED

Newcastle's players and manager Glenn Roeder reacted positively to James's return for the 2006–07 season. He was a starter in the Newcastle side for the entire season.

James displayed his ability to play comfortably in a range of positions by scoring and setting up goals with both feet from both sides. As a result, he signed a new contract at in January, which meant he would stay with the club until 2011. He signed another 4 year contract in May 2007, when Sam Allardyce took over as manager. James said later in the year that he was happy about his future at the club and its new manager saying that training sessions were "the best since I have been here". Big Sam said during the season that James was so keen to play, that he was concerned he would "burn out mentally and physically". As a result, Milner played mainly as a sub in the early part of the season.

After missing the final 9 games of the season due to a foot injury, it was rumoured in May 2008 that he would be part of a transfer to Liverpool. Despite starting the season for Newcastle and scoring in a League Cup win over Coventry, it was revealed after the game that

James had handed in a written transfer request the week before. Super James signed for Villa on the 29th August 2008 for a fee of £12m and signed a 4-year contract with the club.

Return to Aston Villa

James made his debut for us on the 31st August 2008 as a 2nd half sub against Liverpool. His first goals in his second spell came in the FA Cup 3rd Round against Gillingham away on the 4th January 2009 which was his 23rd birthday, where he scored both goals in a 2–1 win for Villa.

James's first Prem goal in his second spell came on the 17th January 2009 against Sunderland Away. He headed in a cross from Young to level for us at 1–1, we went on to win 2–1.

On 7th February 2009, he was named in the England Squad for the first time, after a run of games that had impressed Fabio Capello. James continued to impress and scored his second league goal of the season against Blackburn. He later scored a free-kick from outside the penalty area at home against Everton as Villa came back from 3-1 down to draw us level at 3–3, that was a massive game for us in the fight to try to break into the Champions League and it was in the period when we couldn't win a game. James stated that his time at Villa is his "most settled" period of his career, having played under 13 managers and caretakers despite being only 23.

In season 2009/10, James started playing in central midfield as Stewart Downing came back from injury and Ashley Young played on the right, it was great for James as we all know he can play a lot of different positions and he scored a few in a row so it didn't take him long to adapt. He scored a right screamer at Sunderland and made his debut for the full national team against Holland in August 2009.

Personal View

One of my favourite all-time Villa players Milner's work rate is phenomenal, he is a great passer and scores a lot of good goals and now takes our Penalty's along with John Carew as Young missed a few in a row. He is so energetic and never gives up, he is the type of Villa player all us fans love. I really hope he stays for many years to come and help us break into the Premier League elite.

VILLA HISTORY & BACKGROUND

Club: Aston Villa FC
Formed: 1874
Nickname: The Villains
Colours: Claret and sky blue
Stadium: Villa Park (42,584)
Address: Trinity Rd, Villa Park, Birmingham, B6 6HE
Official website: www.avfc.co.uk

Formed in 1874 by cricketers from the Villa Cross Wesleyan Chapel in the Aston area of Birmingham - hence the name! Founder members of the Football League in 1888, by the turn of the century Villa had won the league championship four times and the FA Cup twice. But following their sixth title triumph in 1910, the club stagnated and had to wait until 1981 for their next championship. But this was Villa's golden period, and in 1982 came the club's greatest achievement - winning the European Cup.

But the heady days were not to last, and since then Villa have only tasted success in the 1994 League Cup. Now it's up to David O'Leary to lift Villa from mid-table mediocrity to a station befitting that of the biggest club in England's second city.

Fact: Villa legend David Platt was once the world's most expensive footballer, his combined transfer fees topping 22million pounds.

Fact: Founded by cricketers, Villa played its first game against Aston Brook St Mary's Rugby team and the game consisted in one half of football and the other of rugby.

ASTON VILLA HISTORY

Founded: 1874
Professional: 1885
Club Nickname: The Villans, Villa
Previous Grounds:
    1874 Wilson Road
    1876-1897 Wellington Road, Perry Barr
    1897 Villa Park
Ground Capacity: 42,700
Pitch Measurements: 115yd x 72yd
Record Attendance:
76,588 v Derby County, FA Cup 6th Rd, 2nd March 1946
Record Transfer Paid:
£9.5m for Juan Pablo Angel to River Plate, December 2000
Record Transfer Received:
£12.6m for Dwight Yorke from Manchester United, August 1998
League Scoring Record:
Tom 'Pongo' Waring 49 Division 1, 1930-31

ASTON VILLA FOOTBALL FOUNDATION

Members of the Aston Villa Wesleyan church formed Villa in 1874 and the team were one of the twelve founder members of the football league in 1888. By this stage they had already won their first trophy with an FA Cup victory in 1887 and they dominated the early league winning the championship 5 times in its first 12 seasons. 1897 was Villa's highpoint as they became double winners.

Most of Aston Villa's history has been spent in the top division but top level success was only found in the Cup competitions until 1981 when they caused a major shock by taking their first league championship for more than 70 years. This was followed up by a European Cup win the following season. Graham Taylor took Villa close to another title in 1990 and they again finished second in 1993's inaugural Premier League, though they have struggled to match that performance since.

There have been a number of League Cup finals and successes, but Villa have never come close to finishing up near the top of the league under the likes of Ron Atkinson, Brian Little or John Gregory. Taylor's return in 2002 proved to be a mistake as he only just managed to save the club from relegation, and he stepped aside at the end of the season. David O'Leary followed him, but couldn't turn the tide and was sacked in the summer of 2006. He was replaced by Martin O'Neill, and that summer also saw the arrival of US businessman Randy Lerner, who bought the club from Doug Ellis.

19th September 2006 was a truly historic day for the villa, here is the stock exchange statement ...

Following the recommended cash offer for Aston Villa plc made by Reform Acquisitions Limited on 14 August 2006, Douglas Ellis OBE, the executive chairman of aston villa, and mr Stephen Kind, Mr Anthony Hales, Mr David Owen and Mr Peter Ellis, non executive directors of Aston Villa, have each resigned from board of directors of aston villa with effect from today, Steve Stride remains an executive director on the board of aston villa.

Aston villa is pleased to announce the appointment of Randolph Lerner as chairman and general Charles c krulak, bob kain and Michael martin as new Non-executive directors. The appointments are effective from today.

CLUB HONOURS

EUROPEAN CUP WINNERS: 1982.

EUROPEAN SUPER CUP WINNERS: 1982-1983.

INTERTOTO CUP WINNERS: 2001.

FOOTBALL LEAGUE CHAMPIONS: 1893-94, 1895-1896, 1896-1897, 1898-1899, 1899-1900, 1909-10, 1980-1981.

FOOTBALL LEAGUE RUNNERS-UP: 1888-89, 1902-03, 1907-08, 1910-11, 1912-13, 1913-1914, 1930-31, 1932-33, 1989-90.

PREMIER LEAGUE RUNNERS-UP: 1992-93.

SECOND DIVISION CHAMPIONS: 1937-1938, 1959-1960.

SECOND DIVISION RUNNERS-UP: 1974-75, 1987-88.

THIRD DIVISION CHAMPIONS: 1971-72.

FA CUP WINNERS: 1887, 1895, 1897, 1905, 1913, 1920, 1957.

FA CUP RUNNERS-UP: 1892, 1924, 2000.

LEAGUE CUP WINNERS: 1961, 1975, 1977, 1994, 1996.

LEAGUE CUP RUNNERS-UP: 1963, 1971.

FA YOUTH CUP WINNERS: 1972, 1980, 2002.

ASTON VILLA v. BIRMINGHAM CITY

	VILLA Wins	Draws	BLUES wins
League	44	27	36
FA Cup	2	1	0
League Cup	4	1	1
Total	50	29	37

2009/10
English Premier   13-09-2009   Birmingham City   0-1 Aston Villa
2007/2008
English Premier   20-04-2008   Aston Villa   5-1 Birmingham City
English Premier   11-11-2007   Birmingham City   1-2 Aston Villa
2005/2006
English Premier   16-04-2006   Aston Villa   3-1 Birmingham City
English Premier   16-10-2005   Birmingham City   0-1 Aston Villa
2004/2005
English Premier   20-03-2005   Birmingham City   2-0 Aston Villa
English Premier   12-12-2004   Aston Villa   1-2 Birmingham City
2003/2004
English Premier   22-02-2004   Aston Villa   2-2 Birmingham City
English Premier   19-10-2003   Birmingham City   0-0 Aston Villa
2002/2003
English Premier   03-03-2003   Aston Villa   0-2 Birmingham City
English Premier   16-09-2002   Birmingham City   3-0 Aston Villa
1993/1994
English League Cup   06-10-1993   Aston Villa   1-0 Birmingham City
English League Cup   21-09-1993   Birmingham City   0-1 Aston Villa
1988/1989
English League Cup   12-10-1988   Aston Villa   5-0 Birmingham City
English League Cup   27-09-1988   Birmingham City   0-2 Aston Villa
1987/1988
English Division 2 (old) 12-12-1987   Birmingham City   1-2 Aston Villa
English Division 2 (old) 22-08-1987   Aston Villa   0-2 Birmingham City
1985/1986
English Division 1 (old) 22-03-1986   Aston Villa   0-3 Birmingham City
English Division 1 (old) 07-09-1985   Birmingham City   0-0 Aston Villa
1983/1984
English Division 1 (old) 31-03-1984   Birmingham City   2-1 Aston Villa
English Division 1 (old) 15-10-1983   Aston Villa   1-0 Birmingham City
1982/1983
English Division 1 (old) 04-04-1983   Aston Villa   1-0 Birmingham City
English Division 1 (old) 27-12-1982   Birmingham City   3-0 Aston Villa

THE VILLA PREMIER YEARS - 1992-2010

1981/1982
ENGLISH DIVISION 1 (OLD)	20-02-1982	BIRMINGHAM CITY	0-1	ASTON VILLA
ENGLISH DIVISION 1 (OLD)	26-09-1981	ASTON VILLA	0-0	BIRMINGHAM CITY

1980/1981
ENGLISH DIVISION 1 (OLD)	13-12-1980	ASTON VILLA	3-0	BIRMINGHAM CITY
ENGLISH DIVISION 1 (OLD)	11-10-1980	BIRMINGHAM CITY	1-2	ASTON VILLA

1978/1979
ENGLISH DIVISION 1 (OLD)	03-03-1979	ASTON VILLA	1-0	BIRMINGHAM CITY
ENGLISH DIVISION 1 (OLD)	21-10-1978	BIRMINGHAM CITY	0-1	ASTON VILLA

1977/1978
ENGLISH DIVISION 1 (OLD)	25-02-1978	BIRMINGHAM CITY	1-0	ASTON VILLA
ENGLISH DIVISION 1 (OLD)	01-10-1977	ASTON VILLA	0-1	BIRMINGHAM CITY

1976/1977
ENGLISH DIVISION 1 (OLD)	10-05-1977	BIRMINGHAM CITY	2-1	ASTON VILLA
ENGLISH DIVISION 1 (OLD)	18-09-1976	ASTON VILLA	1-2	BIRMINGHAM CITY

1975/1976
ENGLISH DIVISION 1 (OLD)	03-04-1976	BIRMINGHAM CITY	3-2	ASTON VILLA
ENGLISH DIVISION 1 (OLD)	27-09-1975	ASTON VILLA	2-1	BIRMINGHAM CITY

1969/1970
ENGLISH DIVISION 2 (OLD)	30-03-1970	BIRMINGHAM CITY	0-2	ASTON VILLA
ENGLISH DIVISION 2 (OLD)	18-10-1969	ASTON VILLA	0-0	BIRMINGHAM CITY

1968/1969
ENGLISH DIVISION 2 (OLD)	12-04-1969	ASTON VILLA	1-0	BIRMINGHAM CITY
ENGLISH DIVISION 2 (OLD)	21-09-1968	BIRMINGHAM CITY	4-0	ASTON VILLA

1967/1968
ENGLISH DIVISION 2 (OLD)	24-02-1968	BIRMINGHAM CITY	2-1	ASTON VILLA
ENGLISH DIVISION 2 (OLD)	07-10-1967	ASTON VILLA	2-4	BIRMINGHAM CITY

1964/1965
ENGLISH DIVISION 1 (OLD)	12-04-1965	ASTON VILLA	3-0	BIRMINGHAM CITY
ENGLISH DIVISION 1 (OLD)	13-02-1965	BIRMINGHAM CITY	0-1	ASTON VILLA

1963/1964
ENGLISH DIVISION 1 (OLD)	31-03-1964	BIRMINGHAM CITY	3-3	ASTON VILLA
ENGLISH DIVISION 1 (OLD)	30-03-1964	ASTON VILLA	0-3	BIRMINGHAM CITY

1962/1963
ENGLISH LEAGUE CUP	27-05-1963	ASTON VILLA	0-0	BIRMINGHAM CITY
ENGLISH LEAGUE CUP	23-05-1963	BIRMINGHAM CITY	3-1	ASTON VILLA
ENGLISH DIVISION 1 (OLD)	16-03-1963	ASTON VILLA	4-0	BIRMINGHAM CITY
ENGLISH DIVISION 1 (OLD)	27-10-1962	BIRMINGHAM CITY	3-2	ASTON VILLA

1961/1962
ENGLISH DIVISION 1 (OLD)	17-03-1962	BIRMINGHAM CITY	0-2	ASTON VILLA
ENGLISH DIVISION 1 (OLD)	28-10-1961	ASTON VILLA	1-3	BIRMINGHAM CITY

1960/1961
ENGLISH DIVISION 1 (OLD)	11-03-1961	BIRMINGHAM CITY	1-1	ASTON VILLA
ENGLISH DIVISION 1 (OLD)	22-10-1960	ASTON VILLA	6-2	BIRMINGHAM CITY

1958/1959
ENGLISH DIVISION 1 (OLD)	20-12-1958	BIRMINGHAM CITY	4-1	ASTON VILLA
ENGLISH DIVISION 1 (OLD)	23-08-1958	ASTON VILLA	1-1	BIRMINGHAM CITY

1957/1958
ENGLISH DIVISION 1 (OLD)	21-12-1957	ASTON VILLA	0-2	BIRMINGHAM CITY

THE VILLA PREMIER YEARS - 1992-2010

English Division 1 (old)	24-08-1957	Birmingham City	3-1	Aston Villa
1956/1957				
English Division 1 (old)	10-04-1957	Birmingham City	1-2	Aston Villa
English Division 1 (old)	27-10-1956	Aston Villa	3-1	Birmingham City
1955/1956				
English Division 1 (old)	21-09-1955	Birmingham City	2-2	Aston Villa
English Division 1 (old)	05-09-1955	Aston Villa	0-0	Birmingham City
1949/1950				
English Division 1 (old)	29-04-1950	Birmingham City	2-2	Aston Villa
English Division 1 (old)	10-12-1949	Aston Villa	1-1	Birmingham City
1948/1949				
English Division 1 (old)	30-04-1949	Birmingham City	0-1	Aston Villa
English Division 1 (old)	04-12-1948	Aston Villa	0-3	Birmingham City
1938/1939				
English Division 1 (old)	04-03-1939	Aston Villa	5-1	Birmingham City
English Division 1 (old)	29-10-1938	Birmingham City	3-0	Aston Villa
1935/1936				
English Division 1 (old)	28-03-1936	Aston Villa	2-1	Birmingham City
English Division 1 (old)	23-11-1935	Birmingham City	2-2	Aston Villa
1934/1935				
English Division 1 (old)	29-12-1934	Aston Villa	2-2	Birmingham City
English Division 1 (old)	25-08-1934	Birmingham City	2-1	Aston Villa
1933/1934				
English Division 1 (old)	14-04-1934	Aston Villa	1-1	Birmingham City
English Division 1 (old)	02-12-1933	Birmingham City	0-0	Aston Villa
1932/1933				
English Division 1 (old)	08-03-1933	Birmingham City	3-2	Aston Villa
English Division 1 (old)	22-10-1932	Aston Villa	1-0	Birmingham City
1931/1932				
English Division 1 (old)	02-04-1932	Birmingham City	1-1	Aston Villa
English Division 1 (old)	21-11-1931	Aston Villa	3-2	Birmingham City
1930/1931				
English Division 1 (old)	21-02-1931	Birmingham City	0-4	Aston Villa
English Division 1 (old)	18-10-1930	Aston Villa	1-1	Birmingham City
1929/1930				
English Division 1 (old)	28-12-1929	Birmingham City	1-1	Aston Villa
English Division 1 (old)	31-08-1929	Aston Villa	2-1	Birmingham City
1928/1929				
English Division 1 (old)	09-03-1929	Aston Villa	1-2	Birmingham City
English Division 1 (old)	27-10-1928	Birmingham City	2-4	Aston Villa
1927/1928				
English Division 1 (old)	17-03-1928	Aston Villa	1-1	Birmingham City
English Division 1 (old)	05-11-1927	Birmingham City	1-1	Aston Villa
1926/1927				
English Division 1 (old)	19-03-1927	Aston Villa	4-2	Birmingham City
English Division 1 (old)	30-10-1926	Birmingham City	1-2	Aston Villa
1925/1926				
English Division 1 (old)	27-02-1926	Birmingham City	2-1	Aston Villa
English Division 1 (old)	17-10-1925	Aston Villa	3-3	Birmingham City

THE VILLA PREMIER YEARS - 1992-2010

1924/1925
English Division 1 (old)	14-02-1925	Aston Villa	1-0	Birmingham City
English Division 1 (old)	11-10-1924	Birmingham City	1-0	Aston Villa

1923/1924
English Division 1 (old)	01-09-1923	Aston Villa	0-0	Birmingham City
English Division 1 (old)	25-08-1923	Birmingham City	3-0	Aston Villa

1922/1923
English Division 1 (old)	24-03-1923	Aston Villa	3-0	Birmingham City
English Division 1 (old)	17-03-1923	Birmingham City	1-0	Aston Villa

1921/1922
English Division 1 (old)	15-03-1922	Birmingham City	1-0	Aston Villa
English Division 1 (old)	11-03-1922	Aston Villa	1-1	Birmingham City

1907/1908
English Division 1 (old)	18-01-1908	Aston Villa	2-3	Birmingham City
English Division 1 (old)	21-09-1907	Birmingham City	2-3	Aston Villa

1906/1907
English Division 1 (old)	19-01-1907	Birmingham City	3-2	Aston Villa
English Division 1 (old)	15-09-1906	Aston Villa	4-1	Birmingham City

1905/1906
English Division 1 (old)	20-01-1906	Aston Villa	1-3	Birmingham City
English Division 1 (old)	16-09-1905	Birmingham City	2-0	Aston Villa

1904/1905
English Division 1 (old)	25-02-1905	Birmingham City	0-3	Aston Villa
English Division 1 (old)	29-10-1904	Aston Villa	2-1	Birmingham City

1903/1904
English Division 1 (old)	16-01-1904	Aston Villa	1-1	Birmingham City
English Division 1 (old)	19-09-1903	Birmingham City	2-2	Aston Villa

1901/1902
English Division 1 (old)	26-12-1901	Aston Villa	1-0	Birmingham City
English Division 1 (old)	12-10-1901	Birmingham City	0-2	Aston Villa

1900/1901
English FA Cup	27-03-1901	Aston Villa	1-0	Birmingham City
English FA Cup	23-03-1901	Birmingham City	0-0	Aston Villa

1895/1896
English Division 1 (old)	26-10-1895	Birmingham City	1-4	Aston Villa
English Division 1 (old)	07-09-1895	Aston Villa	7-3	Birmingham City

1894/1895
English Division 1 (old)	20-10-1894	Birmingham City	2-2	Aston Villa
English Division 1 (old)	01-09-1894	Aston Villa	2-1	Birmingham City

1887/1888
English FA Cup	05-11-1887	Aston Villa	4-0	Birmingham City

VILLA'S PLAYER SQUAD LISTS 1992-2010

1992-93

Aston, Lee
Atkinson, Dalian
Bailey, Russell
Barrett, Earl
Barrett, Neil
Beeck, Christian
Beinlich, Stefan
Berry, Trevor
Blake, Mark
Blenkenship, Paul
Boden, Christopher
Bosnich, Mark
Boxall, Michael
Breitkreutz, Matthias
Brock, Stuart
Brown, Ian
Browne, Paul
Bunbury, Alex
Burchell, Lee
Byfield, Darren
Carruthers, Martin
Collins, Lee
Cowe, Steven
Cox, Neil
Crisp, Richard
Cullen, Tony
Daley, Anthony
Davis, Mike
Davis, Neil
Donnelly, Steve
Ehiogu, Ugochuku
Evans, Darren
Evans, Paul

Farrell, David
Farrelly, Gareth
Fenton, Graham
Finney, Nicholas
Froggatt, Stephen
Gillhaus, Hans
Goodwin, Craig
Harrison, Garry
Henderson, Brian
Henderson, I.
Hendrie, Lee
Hines, Leslie
Hodgson, Shaun
Houghton, Raymond
Hutson, Otis
Jaszczun, Antony
King, Ian
Kubicki, Dariusz
Larsen, Henrik
Leek, Brian
Livingstone, Glen
McAvennie, Frank
McCallum, Matthew
McGrath, Paul
McGuiness, Joe
McLaughlin, Scott
McNamara, Phillip
Miley, Jonathan
Mitchell, Andrew
Moore, David
Murphy, John
Nagbe, Joe
Oakes, Michael

THE VILLA PREMIER YEARS - 1992-2010

Parker, Garry
Pearce, Christopher
Pearce, Dennis
Peters, Mark
Petty, Ben
Pitcher, Steven
Pugh, Mark
Rachel, Adam
Regis, Cyrille
Richardson, Kevin
Ryan, John
Saunders, Dean
Scalley,
Scimeca, Riccardo
Sealey, Leslie
Senior, Marc
Shaw, Gareth
Small, Bryan
Spink, Nigel
Staunton, Stephen
Staunton, Tommy
Teale, Shaun
Thomas, Martin
Williams, Graeme
Williams, Lee
Wiltshire, John
Yorke, Dwight

1993-94.

Abdellah, Nacer
Appleby, Mark
Aston, Lee
Atkinson, Dalian
Barrett, Earl
Barrett, Neil
Berry, Trevor
Blackwood, Michael
Boden, Christopher
Bosnich, Mark
Brock, Stuart
Brown, Ian
Browne, Paul
Burchell, Lee
Burgess, Richard
Byfield, Darren
Carr, Franz
Charles, Gary
Collins, Lee
Cowe, Steven
Davis, Neil
Deacon, Robert
Ehiogu, Ugochuku
Evans, Darren
Farrell, David
Farrelly, Gareth
Fashanu, John
Fenton, Graham
Freestone,
George, Matthew
Hadland, Guy
Halliday, James
Hazell, Reuben
Hendrie, Lee
Hickman, John
Hines, Leslie
Hoop, Ronald
Houghton, Raymond
Hughes, David
Hutchings,
Impey, James
Jaszczun, Antony

Johnson, Tommy
Jones, Jonathan
Jones, Mark
King, Phillip
Kirby, Alan
Lamptey, Nii
Lee, Alan
Lescott, Aaron
Lonsdale, David
McGrath, Paul
Michael,
Middleton, Darren
Miles, Nicholas
Miley, Jonathan
Mitchell, Andrew
Mooney, Darrell
Moore, David
Murphy, John
Murray, Scott
Oakes, Michael
Parker, Garry
Pearce, Dennis
Peters, Mark

Petty, Ben
Rachel, Adam
Read, Lewis
Reece, Dominic
Richardson, Kevin
Saunders, Dean
Scimeca, Riccardo
Senior, Marc
Serrie, David
Small, Bryan
Spink, Nigel
Staunton, Stephen
Tallentire,
Taylor, Ian
Teale, Shaun
Townsend, Andrew
Walker, Richard
West, Daniel
Whittingham, Guy
Wright, Alan
Yorke, Dwight

1994-95

Aston, Lee
Atkinson, Dalian
Barrett, Earl
Barrett, Neil
Beinlich, Stefan
Berry, Trevor
Blenkenship, Paul
Bluck,
Boden, Christopher
Bosnich, Mark
Bowler,
Boxall, Michael

Breitkreutz, Matthias
Brock, Stuart
Brown, Ian
Browne, Paul
Burchell, Lee
Burgess, Richard
Byfield, Darren
Chaliner,
Coles,
Collins, Lee
Coulter,
Cowans, Gordon

THE VILLA PREMIER YEARS - 1992-2010

Cowe, Steven
Cox, Neil
Crawford,
Crisp, Richard
Cross,
Daley, Anthony
Davis, Neil
Deacon, Robert
Devlin,
Doherty,
Dunn,
Ehiogu, Ugochuku
Evans, Darren
Farrell, David
Farrelly, Gareth
Fenton, Graham
Froggatt, Stephen
Glover,
Harrison, Garry
Henderson, Brian
Hendrie, Lee
Hickman, John
Hines, Leslie
Houghton, Raymond
Hughes, David
Impey, James
Jaszczun, Antony
Jones, Jonathan
Kearn,
Kelly,
King, Ian
King, Robert
Kubicki, Dariusz
Lonsdale, David
McAuley, Hugh
McGrath, Paul
Miles, Nicholas
Miley, Jonathan
Mitchell, Andrew
Mooney, Darrell
Moore, David
Murphy, John
Murray, Scott
Oakes, Michael
Parker, Garry
Pearce, Christopher
Pearce, Dennis
Peet, David
Peters, Mark
Petty, Ben
Pitcher, Steven
Rachel, Adam
Ramsey,
Read, Lewis
Richardson, Kevin
Saunders, Dean
Scimeca, Riccardo
Senior, Marc
Small, Bryan
Spink, Nigel
Staunton, Stephen
Teale, Shaun
Townsend, Andrew
Walker, Richard
West, Daniel
Whittingham, Guy
Williams, Lee
Yorke, Dwight

1995-96

Accardi, Giuseppe
Appleby, Mark
Bennett, Dean
Berry, Trevor
Blackwood, Michael
Bosnich, Mark
Brock, Stuart
Browne, Paul
Burchell, Lee
Burgess, Richard
Byfield, Darren
Caricola, Nicola
Carr, Franz
Charles, Gary
Collins, Lee
Cowe, Steven
Davis, Neil
Draper, Mark
Ehiogu, Ugochuku
Elias, Philip
Evans, Allan
Farrell, David
Farrelly, Gareth
Fenton, Graham
George, Matthew
Gregory, John
Guandouzi,
Hadland, Guy
Halliday, James
Harvey, Nathan
Hazell, Reuben
Hendrie, Lee
Hickman, John
Hines, Leslie
Hughes, David
Impey, James
Jaszczun, Antony
Joachim, Julian
Johnson, Tommy
Jones, Mark
King, Phillip
Kirby, Alan
Lambert,
Lee, Alan
Lescott, Aaron
MacDonald, Kevin
McGrath, Paul
Middleton, Darren
Miley, Jonathan
Milosevic, Savo
Mitchell, Andrew
Moore, David
Murray, Scott
Oakes, Michael
Oliver,
Pacheco, Antonio
Petty, Ben
Rachel, Adam
Reece, Dominic
Richards, Danny
Scimeca, Riccardo
Senior, Marc
Small, Bryan
Southgate, Gareth
Spink, Nigel
Staunton, Stephen
Taylor, Ian
Tiler, Carl

Tongue, Philip
Townsend, Andrew
Vassell, Darius
Walker, Richard

Wright, Alan
Yorke, Dwight

1996-97

Apleby, Mark
Barry, Gareth
Blackburn, Bradley
Blackwood, Michael
Bosnich, Mark
Brayley, Albert
Britton, Jonathan
Brock, Stuart
Brown, Christopher
Bull, Nikki
Burchell, Lee
Burgess, Richard
Burke,
Byfield, Darren
Camero, Nelson
Carr, Franz
Charles, Gary
Collins, Lee
Court, David
Crowe, Michael
Curcic, Sasa
Davis, Neil
Draper, Mark
Ehiogu, Ugochuku
Elias, Philip
Evans, Stephen
Farrelly, Gareth
Folds, Liam
George, Matthew
Ghent, Matthew
Hadland, Guy

Halliday, James
Harding, David
Harvey, Nathan
Hazell, Reuben
Hendrie, Lee
Hickman, John
Hines, Leslie
Hughes, David
Jaszczun, Antony
Joachim, Julian
Johnson, Tommy
Kearns, James
Keegan, Justin
King, Phillip
Kirby, Alan
Lee, Alan
Lescott, Aaron
McDonald, Marcus
McGinley,
McGrath, Paul
Matthewman, Scott
Melaugh, Gavin
Meredith, Alex
Middleton, Darren
Miley, Jonathan
Milosevic, Savo
Mulholland, Brian
Murray, Scott
Nelson, Fernando
Oakes, Michael
Petty, Ben

Price, Michael
Prince, Luke
Pulisciano, Nathan
Rachel, Adam
Reece, Dominic
Reeves, Martin
Ridgway, David
Ridley, Martin
Samuel, Jlloyd
Scimeca, Riccardo
Sheridan, Daragh
Sinden, Richard
Southgate, Gareth
Standing, Michael

Staunton, Stephen
Stock, Stephen
Taylor, Ian
Thornley, Stuart
Tiler, Carl
Tongue, Philip
Townsend, Andrew
Vassell, Darius
Walker, Richard
Warren, David
Wickett, Neil
Williams, Joseph
Wright, Alan
Yorke, Dwight

1997-98

Appleby, Mark
Bank,
Barry, Gareth
Bell, Liam
Berks, David
Bewers, Jonathan
Blackburn, Bradley
Blackwood, Michael
Bosnich, Mark
Britton, Jonathan
Bull, Nikki
Byfield, Darren
Charles, Gary
Collins, Lee
Collymore, Stanley
Court, David
Crichton, Paul
Curcic, Sasa
Curtolo, David
Davenport, Calum
Davis, Neil
Draper, Mark

Ehiogu, Ugochuku
Elias, Philip
Evans, Stephen
Folds, Liam
George, Matthew
Ghent, Matthew
Grayson, Simon
Hadland, Guy
Hahnemann, Marcus
Halliday, James
Hansson, Christian
Harding, David
Hazell, Reuben
Hendrie, Lee
Hines, Leslie
Hughes, David
Ilic, Sasa
Impey, Daniel
Jackson, Ben
Jaszczun, Antony
Joachim, Julian
Kearns, James

THE VILLA PREMIER YEARS - 1992-2010

Kirby, Alan
Lee, Alan
Lescott, Aaron
McConnell, Peter
McSeveney, Gary
Melaugh, Gavin
Meredith, Alex
Middleton, Darren
Milosevic, Savo
Mulholland, Brian
Murray, Scott
Myhill, Boaz
Nebrelius, Henrik
Nelson, Fernando
Oakes, Michael
Pavey, Kenny
Petty, Ben
Price, Michael
Prince, Luke
Prosser, Owain
Pulisciano, Ashley
Pulisciano, Nathan
Rachel, Adam
Reece, Dominic
Reeves, Martin
Rhule, Jonathan
Ridley, Martin
Roberts, Matthew

Rotevatn, Anders
Ryan, Jordan
Samuel, Jlloyd
Scimeca, Riccardo
Sheridan, Daragh
Shore, Jamie
Smallman, J.
Smith, Jay
Southgate, Gareth
Standing, Michael
Staunton, Stephen
Stewart, Jordan
Stock, Stephen
Taylor, Ian
Thornley, Stuart
Tiatto, Danny
Tongue, Philip
Townsend, Andrew
Tranter, Martin
Tucker, Matthew
Vassell, Darius
Walker, Richard
Walters, Gregory
Watson, Anthony
Wood,
Wright, Alan
Yorke, Dwight

1998-99

Amoo, Ryan
Andrewartha, David
Barnes, Neil
Barry, Gareth
Bell, Liam
Berks, David
Bewers, Jonathan
Bhutia, Bhaichung

Blackwood, Michael
Bosnich, Mark
Brooker, Matthew
Bull, Nikki
Byfield, Darren
Calderwood, Colin
Campbell, Dudley
Charles, Gary

THE VILLA PREMIER YEARS - 1992-2010

Collins, Lee
Collymore, Stanley
Cox, Danny
Cunnington, James
Curtolo, David
Davenport, Calum
Davies, Gary
De Bolla, Mark
Delaney, Mark
Draper, Mark
Dublin, Dion
Edwards, Jamie
Edwards, Robert
Ehiogu, Ugochuku
Enckelman, Peter
Evans, Graham
Evans, Stephen
Ferraresi, Fabio
Folds, Liam
Ghent, Matthew
Grayson, Simon
Hahnemann, Marcus
Harding, David
Haynes, Daniel
Hazell, Reuben
Hendrie, Lee
Hines, Leslie
Hughes, David
Husbands, Michael
Hylton, Leon
Jackman, Daniel
Jackson, Ben
Jaszczun, Antony
Joachim, Julian
Johnson, Karl
Kearns, James
Latapy, Russell

Lee, Alan
Lescott, Aaron
Lindgren, Kalle
McArthy, Declan
McCarthy, Craig
McConnell, Peter
McGuire, Lee
McSeveney, Gary
Marfell, Andrew
Marsh, Adam
Meacham, Wesley
Melaugh, Gavin
Meredith, Alex
Merson, Paul
Middleton, Darren
Moore, Stefan
Mulholland, Brian
Myhill, Boaz
Nicolas, Alexis
N'Kubi, Isaac
Oakes, Michael
Pawley, James
Petty, Ben
Poston, Tom
Price, Michael
Prince, Luke
Pulisciano, Nathan
Rachel, Adam
Rhule, Jonathan
Richards, Mark
Ridgewell, Liam
Ridley, Martin
Roberts, Matthew
Rollins, Mark
Ryan, Jordan
Sadique, Abdul
Samuel, Jlloyd

Scimeca, Riccardo
Shannon, Lawerence
Smith, Adam
Smith, Dean
Smith, James
Smith, Jay
Southgate, Gareth
Standing, Michael
Stone, Stephen
Tarrant, Neil
Taylor, Ian
Thompson, Alan
Thornley, Stuart
Tranter, Martin
Unsworth, David
Vassell, Darius
Walker, Richard
Walters, Gregory
Watson, Steve
Wells, Andrew
Wright, Alan
Yorke, Dwight

1999-00

Amoo, Ryan
Anastasiou, Yannis
Andrewartha, David
Barry, Gareth
Bartelt, Gustavo
Berks, David
Bewers, Jonathan
Blackwood, Michael
Boateng, George
Byfield, Darren
Calderwood, Colin
Carbone, Benito
Collymore, Stanley
Cooke, Stephen
Cunnington, James
Curtolo, David
Cutler, Neil
De Bolla, Mark
Delaney, Mark
Di Guiseppe, Marcos
Dillon, Sean
Draper, Mark
Dublin, Dion
Edwards, Robert
Ehiogu, Ugochuku
Enckelman, Peter
Evans, Graham
Evans, Stephen
Fahey, Keith
Folds, Liam
Ghent, Matthew
Ghrayib, Najwan
Harding, David
Haynes, Daniel
Henderson, Wayne
Hendrie, Lee
Hughes, David
Hughes, Robert
Husbands, Michael
Hylton, Leon
Itonga, Cedric
Jackman, Daniel
James, David
Jaszczun, Antony
Joachim, Julian
Johnson, Karl
Karlsen, Morten
Kearns, James

THE VILLA PREMIER YEARS - 1992-2010

Lancaster, Martyn
Lescott, Aaron
Lewis, Stuart
McGrath, John
McGuire, Lee
McSeveney, Gary
Marfell, Andrew
Meacham, Wesley
Melaugh, Gavin
Merson, Paul
Middleton, Darren
Moore, Stefan
Moss, Darren
Mulholland, Brian
Myhill, Boaz
Nicolas, Alexis
N'Kubi, Isaac
Oakes, Michael
Pawley, James
Price, Michael
Prince, Luke
Rachel, Adam

Richardson, Keiron
Ridgewell, Liam
Rundell, Adam
Russo, Marco
Samuel, Jlloyd
Smith, Adam
Smith, Jay
Southgate, Gareth
Standing, Michael
Stone, Stephen
Tarrant, Neil
Taylor, Ian
Thompson, Alan
Thornley, Stuart
Vassell, Darius
Walker, Richard
Walters, Gregory
Watson, Steve
Wells, Andrew
Willets, Benjamin
Wright, Alan

2000-01

Alberink, Maiko
Amoo, Ryan
Andrewartha, David
Angel, Juan Pablo
Atkinson, Mark
Baptist, Adam
Barry, Gareth
Beaumont, James
Benchenaa, Nadir
Berks, David
Bertelsen, Trond Erik
Bewers, Jonathan
Boateng, George

Bridges, Stuart
Cooke, Stephen
Cormell, Scott
Cunnington, James
Curtolo, David
Cutler, Neil
De Bilde, Gilles
De Bolla, Mark
Delaney, Mark
Dillon, Sean
Doyle, Colin
Dublin, Dion
Dyer, Lloyd

THE VILLA PREMIER YEARS - 1992-2010

Edwards, Robert
Ehiogu, Ugochuku
Enckelman, Peter
Ennis, Pierre
Evans, Stephen
Fahey, Keith
Folds, Liam
Ghent, Matthew
Ghrayib, Najwan
Ginola, David
Harittu, Ville
Haynes, Daniel
Henderson, Wayne
Hendrie, Lee
Hitzlsperger, Thomas
Husbands, Michael
Hylton, Leon
Hynes, Peter
Jackman, Daniel
James, David
Joachim, Julian
Johnson, Michael
Jones, Robert
Lescott, Aaron
Lewis, Stuart
Lomski, Jan
McArthur, Duncan
McGrath, John
McGuire, Lee
Malpass, John
Marfell, Andrew
Meade, Danny
Meacham, Wesley
Melaugh, Gavin
Merson, Paul
Milner, Robert
Moore, Luke
Moore, Stefan

Myhill, Boaz
Nicolas, Alexis
Nilis, Luc
Nolan, David
Nunez, Milton
O'Connor, James
Özalan, Alpay
Packer, Andrew
Pawley, James
Pelado, Fernando
Poole, Ryan
Ridgewell, Liam
Samuel, Jlloyd
Samuelsen, Jone
Smith, Adam
Smith, Jay
Southgate, Gareth
Standing, Michael
Staunton, Stephen
Steen, Alexander
Stone, Stephen
Stoor, Fredrik
Stuart, Cameron
Tarrant, Neil
Taylor, Ian
Thompson, Alan
Thornley, Stuart
Vassell, Darius
Walker, Joshua
Walker, Richard
Wells, Andrew
Whittingham, Peter
Willets, Benjamin
Williams, Oliver
Wright, Alan

2001-02

Abildgaard, Casper
Agbonlahor, Gabriel
Amoo, Ryan
Andersson, Stefan
Andrewartha, David
Angel, Juan Pablo
Atkinson, Mark
Balaban, Bosko
Baptist, Adam
Barry, Gareth
Berks, David
Bewers, Jonathan
Boateng, George
Brazil, Alan
Bridges, Daniel
Bridges, Stuart
Cahill, Gary
Caney, Rowan
Christensen, Thomas
Cooke, Stephen
Cormell, Scott
Crouch, Peter
Cunnington, James
Davis, Steven
Delaney, Mark
Dillon, Sean
Dublin, Dion
Edwards, Robert
Elttor, Hjalgrim
Enckelman, Peter
Ennis, Pierre
Eremenko, Aleksei Jr.
Fahey, Keith
Folds, Liam
Foley-Sheridan, Stephen
Gahan, Stephen
Ginola, David
Grady, John
Green, Nick
Green, Paul
Hadji, Mustapha
Haynes, Daniel
Henderson, Wayne
Hendrie, Lee
Hitzlsperger, Thomas
Husbands, Michael
Hylton, Leon
Hynes, Peter
Jackman, Daniel
Kachloul, Hassan
Kandaurov, Sergei
McCombe, Jamie
McGrath, John
McGuire, Lee
Malpass, John
Marfell, Andrew
Marshall, Colin
Melaugh, Gavin
Mellberg, Olof
Merson, Paul
Moore, Luke
Moore, Stefan
Myhill, Boaz
Nicolas, Alexis
Nolan, David
O'Connor, James
Özalan, Alpay
Paul, Shane
Pawley, James
Pecora, Antoni
Ridgewell, Liam
Samuel, Jlloyd

THE VILLA PREMIER YEARS - 1992-2010

SCHMEICHEL, PETER
SCULLION, DAVID
SMITH, JAY
SPERANZA, GIOVANNI
STANDING, MICHAEL
STAUNTON, STEPHEN
STONE, STEPHEN
STUART, CAMERON
TARRANT, NEIL
TAYLOR, IAN

TURNER, JOHN
VASSELL, DARIUS
WALKER, RICHARD
WARD, JAMIE
WELLS, ANDREW
WHITTINGHAM, PETER
WILLETS, BENJAMIN
WILLIAMS, OLIVER
WRIGHT, ALAN

2002-03

AARITALO, MIKA
AGBONLAHOR, GABRIEL
ALLBÄCK, MARCUS
AMOO, RYAN
ANGEL, JUAN PABLO
ATKINSON, MARK
BALABAN, BOSKO
BAPTIST, ADAM
BARRY, GARETH
BEWERS, JONATHAN
BOATENG, GEORGE
BOULDING, MICHAEL
BRAZIL, ALAN
BRIDGES, DANIEL
BRIDGES, STUART
CAHILL, GARY
CANEY, ROWAN
COOKE, STEPHEN
CORMELL, SCOTT
CROUCH, PETER
DAVIS, STEVEN
DE LA CRUZ, ULISES
DELANEY, MARK
DUBLIN, DION
EDKINS, ASHLEY
EDWARDS, ROBERT

ENCKELMAN, PETER
ENNIS, PIERRE
FAHEY, KEITH
FOLEY-SHERIDAN, STEPHEN
GAHAN, STEPHEN
GARDNER, CRAIG
GRADY, JOHN
GRANT, LEE
GREEN, NICK
GREEN, PAUL
GUDJONSSON, JOHANNES
HADJI, MUSTAPHA
HAYNES, DANIEL
HENDERSON, WAYNE
HENDRIE, LEE
HITZLSPERGER, THOMAS
HUSBANDS, MICHAEL
HYLTON, LEON
HYNES, PETER
JACK, KELVIN
JACKMAN, DANIEL
JOHNSEN, RONNY
JONES, STEVE
KABEYA, CHRISTIAN
KACHLOUL, HASSAN
KINSELLA, MARK

Kouman, Amadou
Lagerblom, Lasse
Leonhardsen, Öyvind
Lewis, Matt
McGrath, John
McGuire, Lee
Malpass, John
Marshall, Colin
Masalin, Jon
Melaugh, Gavin
Mellberg, Olof
Meredith, Jake
Merson, Paul
Moore, Luke
Moore, Stefan
Morgan, Oluwaseyi
Mulcahy, Kevin
Myhill, Boaz
Nix, Kyle
Noakes, Michael
Nolan, David
O'Connor, James

Osbourne, Isaiah
Özalan, Alpay
Paul, Shane
Pecora, Antoni
Postma, Stefan
Ridgewell, Liam
Samuel, Jlloyd
Scullion, David
Smith, Jay
Sögård, Espen
Staunton, Stephen
Stone, Stephen
Stuart, Cameron
Taylor, Ian
Vassell, Darius
Ward, Jamie
Whittingham, Peter
Williams, Oliver
Williams, Sam
Wright, Alan
Yarnold, Andrew

2003-04

Aaritalo, Mika
Abshir, Abdiligan
Agbonlahor, Gabriel
Allbäck, Marcus
Allen,
Amoo, Ryan
Angel, Juan Pablo
Balaban, Bosko
Barry, Gareth
Bengelloun, Youness
Ben Haim, Tal
Bewers, Jonathan
Boyle, Lee

Brazil, Alan
Bridges, Scott
Bridges, Stuart
Browne, Kenneth
Cahill, Gary
Caney, Rowan
Cooke, Stephen
Cormell, Scott
Crouch, Peter
Davis, Steven
De la Cruz, Ulises
Delaney, Mark
Demontagnac, Ishmel

THE VILLA PREMIER YEARS - 1992-2010

Dublin, Dion
Edkins, Ashley
Edwards, Robert
Enckelman, Peter
Ennis, Pierre
Evans, Morgan
Foley-Sheridan, Stephen
Gardner, Craig
Grady, John
Grant, Lee
Green, Nick
Green, Paul
Grisales, Freddy
Hadji, Mustapha
Henderson, Wayne
Hendrie, Lee
Hitzlsperger, Thomas
Hughes, Ross
Hynes, Peter
Jackman, Daniel
Johnsen, Ronny
Julien, Nigel
Kabeya, Christian
Kachloul, Hassan
Kilkenny, Neil
Kinsella, Mark
Kouman, Amadou
McCann, Gavin
MacDonald, Daniel
Marshall, Colin
Masalin, Jon
Mellberg, Olof
Meredith, Jake
Moore, Luke
Moore, Stefan
Morgan, Oluwaseyi
Mulcahy, Kevin

Myhill, Boaz
Nix, Kyle
Noakes, Michael
O'Connor, James
O'Halloran, Stephen
Olejnik, Robert
Osbourne, Isaiah
Özalan, Alpay
Paul, Shane
Pecora, Antoni
Phelan,
Postma, Stefan
Reeves, Charlie
Ridgewell, Liam
Sampson, Luke
Samuel, Jlloyd
Saunders, Matthew
Schembri, André
Solano, Nolberto
Sörensen, Thomas
Sztybel, Jay
Taylor, Darryl
Troest, Magnus
Tuohy, Michael
Vassell, Darius
Ward, Jamie
Whittingham, Peter
Williams, Sam
Yarnold, Andrew

2004-05

Aaritalo, Mika
Agbonlahor, Gabriel
Allbäck, Marcus
Angel, Juan Pablo
Baldock, Sam
Barry, Gareth
Berson, Mathieu
Bevan, David
Boyle, Lee
Bridges, Scott
Bridges, Stuart
Cahill, Gary
Caney, Rowan
Carew, Ashley
Cole, Carlton
Collins, Jordan
Cooke, Stephen
Davis, Steven
De la Cruz, Ulises
Delaney, Mark
Djemba-Djemba, Eric
Drobny, Vaclav
Edkins, Ashley
Evans, Morgan
Foley-Sheridan, Stephen
Gardner, Craig
Grant, Lee
Green, Paul
Green, Philip
Henderson, Stephen
Henderson, Wayne
Hendrie, Lee
Herd, Chris
Hitzlsperger, Thomas
Hogg, Jonathan
Jackson, Nathan
Kabeya, Christian
Kelly, John Paul
Kouman, Amadou
Laursen, Martin
Lowry, Shane
McCann, Gavin
MacDonald, Daniel
McGurk, Adam
Malpass, Andrew
Masalin, Jon
Mellberg, Olof
Moore, Luke
Moore, Stefan
Morgan, Oluwaseyi
Mulcahy, Kevin
Nix, Kyle
O'Connor, James
O'Halloran, Stephen
Olejnik, Robert
Osbourne, Isaiah
Paul, Shane
Pittman, Jon-Paul
Postma, Stefan
Ridgewell, Liam
Samuel, Jlloyd
Saunders, Matthew
Solano, Nolberto
Sörensen, Thomas
Troest, Magnus
Tuohy, Michael
Vassell, Darius
Ward, Jamie
Whittingham, Peter
Williams, Sam

2005-06.

Agbonlahor, Gabriel
Albrighton, Marc
Angel, Juan Pablo
Bakke, Eirik
Baroš, Milan
Barry, Gareth
Berger, Patrik
Berson, Mathieu
Bevan, David
Bouma, Wilfred
Boyle, Lee
Bridges, Daniel
Bridges, Scott
Cahill, Gary
Caney, Rowan
Carew, Ashley
Clancy, Steven
Clark, Ciaran
Collins, Jordan
Davis, Steven
De la Cruz, Ulises
Delaney, Mark
Djemba-Djemba, Eric
Earls, Danny
Evans, Morgan
Foley-Sheridan, Stephen
Gardner, Craig
Grant, Lee
Green, Paul
Green, Philip
Henderson, Stephen
Henderson, Wayne
Hendrie, Lee
Herd, Chris
Hogg, Jonathan
Hughes, Aaron
Kabeya, Christian
Laursen, Martin
Lowry, Shane
Lund, Erik
McCann, Gavin
MacDonald, Daniel
McGuire, Lee
McGurk, Adam
Mellberg, Olof
Mikaelsson, Tobias
Milner, James
Moore, Luke
Morgan, Oluwaseyi
Mussell, Lee
O'Halloran, Stephen
Olejnik, Robert
Osbourne, Isaiah
Parish, Elliot
Paul, Shane
Phillips, Kevin
Postma, Stefan
Reid, Reuben
Ridgewell, Liam
Roome, Matthew
Samuel, Jlloyd
Saunders, Matthew
Solano, Nolberto
Sörensen, Thomas
Stieber, Zoltán
Taylor, Stuart
Ward, Jamie
Whittingham, Peter
Williams, Sam

2006-07

- Agathe, Didier
- Agbonlahor, Gabriel
- Albrighton, Marc
- Angel, Juan Pablo
- Bannan, Barry
- Bardsley, Phil
- Baroš, Milan
- Barry, Gareth
- Bellon, Damian
- Bellon, Yago
- Berger, Patrik
- Berson, Mathieu
- Bevan, David
- Bouma, Wilfred
- Boyle, Lee
- Bradley, Daniel
- Bridges, Scott
- Burge, Joshua
- Cahill, Gary
- Carew, John
- Clancy, Steven
- Clark, Ciaran
- Collins, James
- Collins, Jordan
- Davis, Steven
- Delaney, Mark
- Delfouneso, Nathan
- Djemba-Djemba, Eric
- Earls, Danny
- Evans, Morgan
- Flingmark, Jacob
- Gardner, Craig
- Georgiou, Stefanos
- Green, Paul
- Green, Philip
- Griffiths, Aaron
- Henderson, Stephen
- Hendrie, Lee
- Herd, Chris
- Hogg, Jonathan
- Hughes, Aaron
- Kabeya, Christian
- Király, Gábor
- Laursen, Martin
- Love, Ben
- Lowry, Shane
- Lund, Erik
- McCann, Gavin
- MacDonald, Daniel
- McGurk, Adam
- Maloney, Shaun
- Mellberg, Olof
- Mikaelsson, Tobias
- Moore, Luke
- Morgan, Oluwaseyi
- O'Halloran, Stephen
- Olejnik, Robert
- Osbourne, Isaiah
- Panayiotou, Feidias
- Parish, Elliot
- Petrov, Stiliyan
- Phillips, Kevin
- Power, Mark
- Ricketts, Will
- Ridgewell, Liam
- Roome, Matthew
- Samuel, Jlloyd
- Simmonds, Sam
- Söder, Robin
- Sörensen, Thomas
- Staw, Lasse
- Stieber, Zoltán
- Sutton, Chris
- Taylor, Stuart

Whittingham, Peter
Williams, Sam

Young, Ashley

2007-08

Agbonlahor, Gabriel
Albrighton, Marc
Baker, Nathan
Bannan, Barry
Barry, Gareth
Bellon, Damian
Bellon, Yago
Berger, Patrik
Berry, Joel
Bevan, David
Blythe, Richard
Bouma, Wilfred
Boyle, Lee
Bradley, Daniel
Bridges, Scott
Cahill, Gary
Carew, John
Carson, Scott
Chamberlain, Deale
Clancy, Steven
Clark, Ciaran
Clifton, James
Collins, James
Collins, Jordan
Dau, Thomas
Davies, Curtis
Delaney, Mark
Delfouneso, Nathan
Djemba-Djemba, Eric
Dyer, Jack
Earls, Danny
Flanagan, Calum
Forrester, Harry
Gardner, Craig

Gardner, Gary
Griffiths, Aaron
Grocott, William
Gucher, Robert
Harewood, Marlon
Herd, Chris
Heslop, Lance
Hofbauer, Dominik
Hogg, Jonathan
Jackman, Joseph
Knight, Zat
Lampkin, Jason
Laursen, Martin
Lichaj, Eric
Love, Ben
Lowry, Shane
Lund, Erik
McGurk, Adam
Maloney, Shaun
Mandanda, Steve
Mellberg, Olof
Menessou, Arsene
Mikaelsson, Tobias
Moore, Ethan
Moore, Luke
O'Halloran, Stephen
Osbourne, Isaiah
Parish, Elliot
Petrov, Stiliyan
Power, Mark
Poyser, Kofi
Reo-Coker, Nigel
Ricketts, Will
Ridgewell, Liam

Roberts, Tomos
Roome, Matthew
Routledge, Wayne
Salifou, Moustapha
Simmonds, Ryan
Simmonds, Sam
Sörensen, Thomas

Stieber, András
Stieber, Zoltán
Taylor, Stuart
Ward, Charles Patrick
Weimann, Andreas
Williams, Sam
Young, Ashley

2008-09

Agbonlahor, Gabriel
Albrighton, Marc
Baker, Nathan
Bannan, Barry
Barry, Gareth
Berry, Joel
Bevan, David
Blythe, Richard
Bouma, Wilfred
Bradley, Daniel
Carew, John
Clark, Ciaran
Clifton, James
Collins, James
Collins, Jordan
Cuéllar, Carlos
Dau, Thomas
Davies, Curtis
Delfouneso, Nathan
Dyer, Jack
Flanagan, Calum
Forrester, Harry
Friedel, Brad
Gardner, Craig
Gardner, Gary
Grocott, William
Gucher, Robert
Guzan, Brad
Harewood, Marlon

Haxhia, Aldi
Herd, Chris
Heslop, Lance
Hofbauer, Dominik
Hogg, Jonathan
Holtom, Fred
Knight, Zat
Lampkin, Jason
Laursen, Martin
Lichaj, Eric
Love, Ben
Lowry, Shane
McGurk, Adam
Maloney, Shaun
Mikaelsson, Tobias
Milner, James
Moore, Ethan
O'Halloran, Stephen
Osbourne, Isaiah
Parish, Elliot
Petrov, Stiliyan
Power, Mark
Poyser, Kofi
Reo-Coker, Nigel
Ricketts, Will
Roberts, Tomos
Roome, Matthew
Routledge, Wayne
Salifou, Moustapha

THE VILLA PREMIER YEARS - 1992-2010

Shorey, Nicky
Sidwell, Steven
Simmonds, Ryan
Simmonds, Sam
Stieber, András
Stieber, Zoltán

Taylor, Stuart
Ward, Charles Patrick
Weimann, Andreas
Williams, Sam
Young, Ashley
Young, Luke

2009/10

1 Brad Friedel
2 Luke Young
3 Wilfred Bouma
4 Steven Sidwell
5 Richard Dunne
6 Stewart Downing
7 Ashley Young
8 James Milner
10 John Carew
11 Gabriel Agbonlahor
12 Marc Albrighton
14 Nathan Delfouneso
15 Curtis Davies
16 Fabian Delph

17 Moustapha Salifou
18 Emile Heskey
19 Stilian Petrov
20 Nigel Reo-Coker
22 Brad Guzan
23 Habib Beye
24 Carlos Cuellar
25 Stephen Warnock
26 Craig Gardner
29 James Collins
33 Andy Marshall
43 Elliot Parish
47 Claran Clark
Courtney Cameron

Loaned players

Nathan Baker
Barry Bannan
Chris Herd
Nicky Shorey
Marlon Harewood
Isaiah Osbourne
Eric Lichaj
Shane Lowry

1992/1993 RESULTS AND FIXTURES

English Premier	15-08-1992	Ipswich	1-1	**Aston Villa**
English Premier	19-08-1992	**Aston Villa**	1-1	Leeds
English Premier	22-08-1992	**Aston Villa**	1-1	Southampton
English Premier	25-08-1992	Everton	1-0	**Aston Villa**
English Premier	29-08-1992	Sheff Utd	0-2	**Aston Villa**
English Premier	02-09-1992	**Aston Villa**	1-3	Chelsea
English Premier	05-09-1992	**Aston Villa**	3-0	C Palace
English Premier	13-09-1992	Leeds	1-1	Aston Villa
English Premier	19-09-1992	**Aston Villa**	4-2	Liverpool
English Premier	26-09-1992	Middlesbro	2-3	**Aston Villa**
English Premier	03-10-1992	MK Dons	2-3	**Aston Villa**
English Premier	19-10-1992	**Aston Villa**	0-0	Blackburn
English Premier	24-10-1992	Oldham	1-1	**Aston Villa**
English Premier	01-11-1992	**Aston Villa**	2-0	QPR
English Premier	07-11-1992	**Aston Villa**	1-0	Man Utd
English Premier	21-11-1992	Tottenham	0-0	**Aston Villa**
English Premier	28-11-1992	**Aston Villa**	2-3	Norwich
English Premier	05-12-1992	Sheff Wed	1-2	**Aston Villa**
English Premier	12-12-1992	**Aston Villa**	2-1	Nottm Forest
English Premier	19-12-1992	Man City	1-1	**Aston Villa**
English Premier	26-12-1992	Coventry	3-0	**Aston Villa**
English Premier	28-12-1992	**Aston Villa**	1-0	Arsenal
English Premier	09-01-1993	Liverpool	1-2	**Aston Villa**
English Premier	17-01-1993	**Aston Villa**	5-1	Middlesbro
English Premier	27-01-1993	**Aston Villa**	3-1	Sheff Utd
English Premier	30-01-1993	Southampton	2-0	**Aston Villa**
English Premier	06-02-1993	**Aston Villa**	2-0	Ipswich
English Premier	10-02-1993	C Palace	1-0	**Aston Villa**
English Premier	13-02-1993	Chelsea	0-1	**Aston Villa**
English Premier	20-02-1993	**Aston Villa**	2-1	Everton
English Premier	27-02-1993	**Aston Villa**	1-0	MK Dons
English Premier	10-03-1993	**Aston Villa**	0-0	Tottenham
English Premier	14-03-1993	Man Utd	1-1	**Aston Villa**
English Premier	20-03-1993	**Aston Villa**	2-0	Sheff Wed
English Premier	24-03-1993	Norwich	1-0	**Aston Villa**
English Premier	04-04-1993	Nottm Forest	0-1	**Aston Villa**
English Premier	10-04-1993	**Aston Villa**	0-0	Coventry
English Premier	12-04-1993	Arsenal	0-1	**Aston Villa**
English Premier	18-04-1993	**Aston Villa**	3-1	Man City
English Premier	21-04-1993	Blackburn	3-0	**Aston Villa**
English Premier	02-05-1993	**Aston Villa**	0-1	Oldham
English Premier	09-05-1993	QPR	2-1	**Aston Villa**

THE VILLA PREMIER YEARS - 1992-2010

Pos	Club	P	W	D	L	F	A	GD	Pts
1.	Manchester United	42	24	12	6	67	31	36	84
2.	Aston Villa	42	21	11	10	57	40	17	74
3.	Norwich City	42	21	9	12	61	65	-4	72
4.	Blackburn Rovers	42	20	11	11	68	46	22	71
5.	Queens Park Rangers	42	17	12	13	63	55	8	63
6.	Liverpool	42	16	11	15	62	55	7	59
7.	Sheffield Wednesday	42	15	14	13	55	51	4	59
8.	Tottenham Hotspur	42	16	11	15	60	66	-6	59
9.	Manchester City	42	15	12	15	56	51	5	57
10.	Arsenal	42	15	11	16	40	38	2	56
11.	Chelsea	42	14	14	14	51	54	-3	56
12.	Wimbledon	42	14	12	16	56	55	1	54
13.	Everton	42	15	8	19	53	55	-2	53
14.	Sheffield United	42	14	10	18	54	53	1	52
15.	Coventry City	42	13	13	16	52	57	-5	52
16.	Ipswich Town	42	12	16	14	50	55	-5	52
17.	Leeds United	42	12	15	15	57	62	-5	51
18.	Southampton	42	13	11	18	54	61	-7	50
19.	Oldham Athletic	42	13	10	19	63	74	-11	49
20.	Crystal Palace	42	11	16	15	48	61	-13	49
21.	Middlesbrough	42	11	11	20	54	75	-21	44
22.	Nottingham Forest	42	10	10	22	41	62	-21	40

Total
Played	Won	Drawn	Lost	points
42	21 (50 %)	11 (26 %)	10 (24 %)	74

Home
Played	Won	Drawn	Lost	points
21	13 (62 %)	5 (24 %)	3 (14 %)	44

Away
Played	Won	Drawn	Lost	points
21	8 (38 %)	6 (29 %)	7 (33 %)	30

Biggest home win
Jan 17th 1993   Villa   5-1   Middlesbrough

Biggest home loss
Sep 2nd 1992   Villa   1-3   Chelsea
Aug 29th 1992   Sheff. Utd   0-2   Villa

Biggest away loss
Dec 26th 1992   Coventry C.   3-0   Villa
Apr 21st 1993   Blackburn R.   3- 0   Villa

Highest aggregate score home
Sep 19th 1992   Villa   4- 2   Liverpool
Jan 17th 1993   Aston Villa   5- 1   Middlesbrough

Highest aggregate score away
Sep 26th 1992   Middlesbrough   2- 3   Villa
Oct 3rd 1992   Wimbledon   2-3   Villa

THE VILLA PREMIER YEARS - 1992-2010

1993/1994 RESULTS AND FIXTURES

English Premier	14-08-1993	**Aston Villa**	4-1	QPR
English Premier	18-08-1993	Sheff Wed	0-0	**Aston Villa**
English Premier	21-08-1993	MK Dons	2-2	**Aston Villa**
English Premier	23-08-1993	**Aston Villa**	1-2	Man Utd
English Premier	28-08-1993	**Aston Villa**	1-0	Tottenham
English Premier	31-08-1993	Everton	0-1	**Aston Villa**
English Premier	11-09-1993	**Aston Villa**	0-0	Coventry
English Premier	18-09-1993	Ipswich	1-2	**Aston Villa**
English Premier	25-09-1993	Oldham	1-1	**Aston Villa**
English Premier	02-10-1993	**Aston Villa**	0-2	Newcastle
English Premier	16-10-1993	West Ham	0-0	**Aston Villa**
English Premier	23-10-1993	**Aston Villa**	1-0	Chelsea
English Premier	30-10-1993	Swindon	1-2	**Aston Villa**
English Premier	06-11-1993	Arsenal	1-2	**Aston Villa**
English Premier	20-11-1993	**Aston Villa**	1-0	Sheff Utd
English Premier	24-11-1993	**Aston Villa**	0-2	Southampton
English Premier	28-11-1993	Liverpool	2-1	**Aston Villa**
English Premier	04-12-1993	QPR	2-2	**Aston Villa**
English Premier	08-12-1993	**Aston Villa**	2-2	Sheff Wed
English Premier	11-12-1993	**Aston Villa**	0-1	MK Dons
English Premier	19-12-1993	Man Utd	3-1	**Aston Villa**
English Premier	29-12-1993	Norwich	1-2	**Aston Villa**
English Premier	01-01-1994	**Aston Villa**	0-1	Blackburn
English Premier	15-01-1994	**Aston Villa**	3-1	West Ham
English Premier	22-01-1994	Chelsea	1-1	**Aston Villa**
English Premier	06-02-1994	**Aston Villa**	1-0	Leeds
English Premier	12-02-1994	**Aston Villa**	5-0	Swindon
English Premier	22-02-1994	**Aston Villa**	0-0	Man City
English Premier	02-03-1994	Tottenham	1-1	**Aston Villa**
English Premier	06-03-1994	Coventry	0-1	**Aston Villa**
English Premier	12-03-1994	**Aston Villa**	0-1	Ipswich
English Premier	16-03-1994	Leeds	2-0	**Aston Villa**
English Premier	19-03-1994	**Aston Villa**	1-2	Oldham
English Premier	30-03-1994	**Aston Villa**	0-0	Everton
English Premier	02-04-1994	Man City	3-0	**Aston Villa**
English Premier	04-04-1994	**Aston Villa**	0-0	Norwich
English Premier	11-04-1994	Blackburn	1-0	**Aston Villa**
English Premier	16-04-1994	Sheff Utd	1-2	**Aston Villa**
English Premier	23-04-1994	**Aston Villa**	1-2	Arsenal
English Premier	27-04-1994	Newcastle	5-1	**Aston Villa**
English Premier	30-04-1994	Southampton	4-1	**Aston Villa**
English Premier	07-05-1994	**Aston Villa**	2-1	Liverpool

THE VILLA PREMIER YEARS - 1992-2010

Pos	Club	P	W	D	L	F	A	GD	Pts
1.	Manchester United	42	27	11	4	80	38	42	92
2.	Blackburn Rovers	42	25	9	8	63	36	27	84
3.	Newcastle United	42	23	8	11	82	41	41	77
4.	Arsenal	42	18	17	7	53	28	25	71
5.	Leeds United	42	18	16	8	65	39	26	70
6.	Wimbledon	42	18	11	13	56	53	3	65
7.	Sheffield Wednesday	42	16	16	10	76	54	22	64
8.	Liverpool	42	17	9	16	59	55	4	60
9.	Queens Park Rangers	42	16	12	14	62	61	1	60
10.	Aston Villa	42	15	12	15	46	50	-4	57
11.	Coventry City	42	14	14	14	43	45	-2	56
12.	Norwich City	42	12	17	13	65	61	4	53
13.	West Ham United	42	13	13	16	47	58	-11	52
14.	Chelsea	42	13	12	17	49	53	-4	51
15.	Tottenham Hotspur	42	11	12	19	54	59	-5	45
16.	Manchester City	42	9	18	15	38	49	-11	45
17.	Everton	42	12	8	22	42	63	-21	44
18.	Southampton	42	12	7	23	49	66	-17	43
19.	Ipswich Town	42	9	16	17	35	58	-23	43
20.	Sheffield United	42	8	18	16	42	60	-18	42
21.	Oldham Athletic	42	9	13	20	42	68	-26	40
22.	Swindon Town	42	5	15	22	47	100	-53	30

Total
Played	Won	Drawn	Lost	points
42	15 (36 %)	12 (29 %)	15 (36 %)	57

Home
Played	Won	Drawn	Lost	points
21	8 (38 %)	5 (24 %)	8 (38 %)	29

Away
Played	Won	Drawn	Lost	points
21	7 (33 %)	7 (33 %)	7 (33 %)	28

Biggest home win
Feb 12th 1994   Aston Villa   5-0   Swindon Town

Biggest home loss
Oct 2nd 1993   Aston Villa   0-2   Newcastle United
Nov 24th 1993   Aston Villa   0-2   Southampton

Biggest away wins
Aug 31st 1993   Everton   0-1   Aston Villa
Sep 18th 1993   Ipswich Town   1-2   Aston Villa
Oct 30th 1993   Swindon Town   1-2   Aston Villa
Nov 6th 1993   Arsenal   1-2   Aston Villa
Dec 29th 1993   Norwich City   1-2   Aston Villa
Mar 6th 1994   Coventry City   0-1   Aston Villa
Apr 16th 1994   Sheffield United   1-2   Aston Villa

Biggest away loss
Apr 27th 1994   Newcastle United   5-1   Aston Villa

Highest aggregate score home
Aug 14th 1993   Aston Villa   4-1   QPR
Feb 12th 1994   Aston Villa   5-0   Swindon Town

Highest aggregate score away
Apr 27th 1994   Newcastle United   5-1   Aston Villa

ASTON VILLA 1994/1995 RESULTS AND FIXTURES

English Premier	20-08-1994	Everton	2-2	**Aston Villa**
English Premier	24-08-1994	**Aston Villa**	1-1	Southampton
English Premier	27-08-1994	**Aston Villa**	1-1	C Palace
English Premier	29-08-1994	Coventry	0-1	**Aston Villa**
English Premier	10-09-1994	**Aston Villa**	2-0	Ipswich
English Premier	17-09-1994	West Ham	1-0	**Aston Villa**
English Premier	24-09-1994	Blackburn	3-1	**Aston Villa**
English Premier	01-10-1994	**Aston Villa**	0-2	Newcastle
English Premier	08-10-1994	Liverpool	3-2	**Aston Villa**
English Premier	15-10-1994	**Aston Villa**	1-1	Norwich
English Premier	22-10-1994	**Aston Villa**	0-2	Nottm Forest
English Premier	29-10-1994	QPR	2-0	**Aston Villa**
English Premier	06-11-1994	**Aston Villa**	1-2	Man Utd
English Premier	09-11-1994	Wimbledon	4-3	**Aston Villa**
English Premier	19-11-1994	Tottenham	3-4	**Aston Villa**
English Premier	27-11-1994	**Aston Villa**	1-1	Sheff Wed
English Premier	03-12-1994	Leicester	1-1	**Aston Villa**
English Premier	10-12-1994	**Aston Villa**	0-0	Everton
English Premier	19-12-1994	Southampton	2-1	**Aston Villa**
English Premier	26-12-1994	Arsenal	0-0	**Aston Villa**
English Premier	28-12-1994	**Aston Villa**	3-0	Chelsea
English Premier	31-12-1994	Man City	2-2	**Aston Villa**
English Premier	02-01-1995	**Aston Villa**	0-0	Leeds
English Premier	14-01-1995	**Aston Villa**	2-1	QPR
English Premier	21-01-1995	Nottm Forest	1-2	**Aston Villa**
English Premier	25-01-1995	**Aston Villa**	1-0	Tottenham
English Premier	04-02-1995	Man Utd	1-0	**Aston Villa**
English Premier	11-02-1995	**Aston Villa**	7-1	Wimbledon
English Premier	18-02-1995	Sheff Wed	1-2	**Aston Villa**
English Premier	22-02-1995	**Aston Villa**	4-4	Leicester
English Premier	25-02-1995	Newcastle	3-1	**Aston Villa**
English Premier	04-03-1995	**Aston Villa**	0-1	Blackburn
English Premier	06-03-1995	**Aston Villa**	0-0	Coventry
English Premier	18-03-1995	**Aston Villa**	0-2	West Ham
English Premier	01-04-1995	Ipswich	0-1	**Aston Villa**
English Premier	04-04-1995	C Palace	0-0	**Aston Villa**
English Premier	15-04-1995	Chelsea	1-0	**Aston Villa**
English Premier	17-04-1995	**Aston Villa**	0-4	Arsenal
English Premier	29-04-1995	Leeds	1-0	**Aston Villa**
English Premier	03-05-1995	**Aston Villa**	1-1	Man City
English Premier	06-05-1995	**Aston Villa**	2-0	Liverpool
English Premier	14-05-1995	Norwich	1-1	**Aston Villa**

THE VILLA PREMIER YEARS - 1992-2010

Pos	Club	P	W	D	L	F	A	GD	Pts
1.	Blackburn Rovers	42	27	8	7	80	39	41	89
2.	Manchester United	42	26	10	6	77	28	49	88
3.	Nottingham Forest	42	22	11	9	72	43	29	77
4.	Liverpool	42	21	11	10	65	37	28	74
5.	Leeds United	42	20	13	9	59	38	21	73
6.	Newcastle United	42	20	12	10	67	47	20	72
7.	Tottenham Hotspur	42	16	14	12	66	58	8	62
8.	Queens Park Rangers	42	17	9	16	61	59	2	60
9.	Wimbledon	42	15	11	16	48	65	-17	56
10.	Southampton	42	12	18	12	61	63	-2	54
11.	Chelsea	42	13	15	14	50	55	-5	54
12.	Arsenal	42	13	12	17	52	49	3	51
13.	Sheffield Wednesday	42	13	12	17	49	57	-8	51
14.	West Ham United	42	13	11	18	44	48	-4	50
15.	Everton	42	11	17	14	44	51	-7	50
16.	Coventry City	42	12	14	16	44	62	-18	50
17.	Manchester City	42	12	13	17	53	64	-11	49
18.	**Aston Villa**	**42**	**11**	**15**	**16**	**51**	**56**	**-5**	**48**
19.	Crystal Palace	42	11	12	19	34	49	-15	45
20.	Norwich City	42	10	13	19	37	54	-17	43
21.	Leicester City	42	6	11	25	45	80	-35	29
22.	Ipswich Town	42	7	6	29	36	93	-57	27

Total
Played	Won	Drawn	Lost	points
42	11 (26 %)	15 (36 %)	16 (38 %)	48

Home
Played	Won	Drawn	Lost	points
21	6 (29 %)	9 (43 %)	6 (29 %)	27

Away
Played	Won	Drawn	Lost	points
21	5 (24 %)	6 (29 %)	10 (48 %)	21

Biggest home win
Feb 11th 1995　　Aston Villa　　　　7-1　　　　Wimbledon

Biggest home loss
Apr 17th 1995　　Aston Villa　　　　0-4　　　　Arsenal

Biggest away win
Aug 29th 1994　　Coventry City　　　0-1　　　　Aston Villa
Nov 19th 1994　　Tottenham H.　　　3-4　　　　Aston Villa
Jan 21st 1995　　Nottingham F.　　　1-2　　　　Aston Villa
Feb 18th 1995　　Sheffield Wed.　　　1-2　　　　Aston Villa
Apr 1st 1995　　　Ipswich Town　　　0-1　　　　Aston Villa

Biggest away loss
Sep 24th 1994　　Blackburn R.　　　 3-1　　　　Aston Villa
Oct 29th 1994　　 QPR　　　　　　　2-0　　　　Aston Villa
Feb 25th 1995　　Newcastle United　3-1　　　　Aston Villa

Highest aggregate score home
Feb 11th 1995　　Aston Villa　　　　7-1　　　　Wimbledon
Feb 22nd 1995　　Aston Villa　　　　4-4　　　　Leicester City

Highest aggregate score away
Nov 9th 1994　　　Wimbledon　　　　4-3　　　　Aston Villa
Nov 19th 1994　　Tottenham H.　　　3-4　　　　Aston Villa

ASTON VILLA 1995/1996 RESULTS AND FIXTURES

English Premier	19-08-1995	**Aston Villa**	3-1	Man Utd
English Premier	23-08-1995	Tottenham	0-1	**Aston Villa**
English Premier	26-08-1995	Leeds	2-0	**Aston Villa**
English Premier	30-08-1995	**Aston Villa**	1-0	Bolton
English Premier	09-09-1995	Blackburn	1-1	**Aston Villa**
English Premier	16-09-1995	**Aston Villa**	2-0	Wimbledon
English Premier	23-09-1995	**Aston Villa**	1-1	Nottm Forest
English Premier	30-09-1995	Coventry	0-3	**Aston Villa**
English Premier	14-10-1995	**Aston Villa**	0-1	Chelsea
English Premier	21-10-1995	Arsenal	2-0	**Aston Villa**
English Premier	28-10-1995	**Aston Villa**	1-0	Everton
English Premier	04-11-1995	West Ham	1-4	**Aston Villa**
English Premier	18-11-1995	**Aston Villa**	1-1	Newcastle
English Premier	20-11-1995	Southampton	0-1	**Aston Villa**
English Premier	25-11-1995	Man City	1-0	**Aston Villa**
English Premier	02-12-1995	**Aston Villa**	1-1	Arsenal
English Premier	10-12-1995	Nottm Forest	1-1	**Aston Villa**
English Premier	16-12-1995	**Aston Villa**	4-1	Coventry
English Premier	23-12-1995	QPR	1-0	**Aston Villa**
English Premier	01-01-1996	Middlesbro	0-2	**Aston Villa**
English Premier	13-01-1996	Man Utd	0-0	**Aston Villa**
English Premier	21-01-1996	**Aston Villa**	2-1	Tottenham
English Premier	31-01-1996	**Aston Villa**	0-2	Liverpool
English Premier	03-02-1996	**Aston Villa**	3-0	Leeds
English Premier	10-02-1996	Bolton	0-2	**Aston Villa**
English Premier	24-02-1996	Wimbledon	3-3	**Aston Villa**
English Premier	28-02-1996	**Aston Villa**	2-0	Blackburn
English Premier	03-03-1996	Liverpool	3-0	**Aston Villa**
English Premier	06-03-1996	**Aston Villa**	3-2	Sheff Wed
English Premier	09-03-1996	**Aston Villa**	4-2	QPR
English Premier	16-03-1996	Sheff Wed	2-0	**Aston Villa**
English Premier	19-03-1996	**Aston Villa**	0-0	Middlesbro
English Premier	06-04-1996	Chelsea	1-2	**Aston Villa**
English Premier	08-04-1996	**Aston Villa**	3-0	Southampton
English Premier	14-04-1996	Newcastle	1-0	**Aston Villa**
English Premier	17-04-1996	**Aston Villa**	1-1	West Ham
English Premier	27-04-1996	**Aston Villa**	0-1	Man City
English Premier	05-05-1996	Everton	1-0	**Aston Villa**

THE VILLA PREMIER YEARS - 1992-2010

Pos	Club	P	W	D	L	F	A	GD	Pts
F1.	Manchester United	38	25	7	6	73	35	38	82
2.	Newcastle United	38	24	6	8	66	37	29	78
3.	Liverpool	38	20	11	7	70	34	36	71
4.	Aston Villa	38	18	9	11	52	35	17	63
5.	Arsenal	38	17	12	9	49	32	17	63
6.	Everton	38	17	10	11	64	44	20	61
7.	Blackburn Rovers	38	18	7	13	61	47	14	61
8.	Tottenham Hotspur	38	16	13	9	50	38	12	61
9.	Nottingham Forest	38	15	13	10	50	54	-4	58
10.	West Ham United	38	14	9	15	43	52	-9	51
11.	Chelsea	38	12	14	12	46	44	2	50
12.	Middlesbrough	38	11	10	17	35	50	-15	43
13.	Leeds United	38	12	7	19	40	57	-17	43
14.	Wimbledon	38	10	11	17	55	70	-15	41
15.	Sheffield Wednesday	38	10	10	18	48	61	-13	40
16.	Coventry City	38	8	14	16	42	60	-18	38
17.	Southampton	38	9	11	18	34	52	-18	38
18.	Manchester City	38	9	11	18	33	58	-25	38
19.	Queens Park Rangers	38	9	6	23	38	57	-19	33
20.	Bolton Wanderers	38	8	5	25	39	71	-32	29

1995/96

Total

Played	Won	Drawn	Lost	points
38	18 (47 %)	9 (24 %)	11 (29 %)	63

Home

Played	Won	Drawn	Lost	points
19	11 (58 %)	5 (26 %)	3 (16 %)	38

Away

Played	Won	Drawn	Lost	points
19	7 (37 %)	4 (21 %)	8 (42 %)	25

THE VILLA PREMIER YEARS - 1992-2010

Biggest home win
Dec 16th 1995	Aston Villa	4-1	Coventry City
Feb 3rd 1996	Aston Villa	3-0	Leeds United
Apr 8th 1996	Aston Villa	3-0	Southampton

Biggest home loss
Jan 31st 1996	Aston Villa	0-2	Liverpool

Biggest away win
Sep 30th 1995	Coventry City	0-3	Aston Villa
Nov 4th 1995	West Ham United	1-4	Aston Villa

Biggest away loss
Mar 3rd 1996	Liverpool	3-0	Aston Villa

Highest aggregate score home
Mar 9th 1996	Aston Villa	4-2	QPR

Highest aggregate score away
Feb 24th 1996	Wimbledon	3-3	Aston Villa

ASTON VILLA 1996/1997 RESULTS AND FIXTURES

English Premier	17-08-1996	Sheff Wed	2-1	**Aston Villa**
English Premier	21-08-1996	**Aston Villa**	1-0	Blackburn
English Premier	24-08-1996	**Aston Villa**	2-0	Derby
English Premier	04-09-1996	Everton	0-1	**Aston Villa**
English Premier	07-09-1996	**Aston Villa**	2-2	Arsenal
English Premier	15-09-1996	Chelsea	1-1	**Aston Villa**
English Premier	21-09-1996	**Aston Villa**	0-0	Man Utd
English Premier	30-09-1996	Newcastle	4-3	**Aston Villa**
English Premier	12-10-1996	Tottenham	1-0	**Aston Villa**
English Premier	19-10-1996	**Aston Villa**	2-0	Leeds
English Premier	26-10-1996	Sunderland	1-0	**Aston Villa**
English Premier	02-11-1996	**Aston Villa**	2-0	Nottm Forest
English Premier	16-11-1996	**Aston Villa**	1-3	Leicester
English Premier	23-11-1996	Coventry	1-2	**Aston Villa**
English Premier	30-11-1996	**Aston Villa**	1-0	Middlesbro
English Premier	04-12-1996	West Ham	0-2	**Aston Villa**
English Premier	07-12-1996	Southampton	0-1	**Aston Villa**
English Premier	22-12-1996	**Aston Villa**	5-0	Wimbledon
English Premier	26-12-1996	**Aston Villa**	0-2	Chelsea
English Premier	28-12-1996	Arsenal	2-2	**Aston Villa**
English Premier	01-01-1997	Man Utd	0-0	**Aston Villa**
English Premier	11-01-1997	**Aston Villa**	2-2	Newcastle
English Premier	18-01-1997	Liverpool	3-0	**Aston Villa**
English Premier	29-01-1997	**Aston Villa**	0-1	Sheff Wed
English Premier	01-02-1997	**Aston Villa**	1-0	Sunderland
English Premier	19-02-1997	**Aston Villa**	2-1	Coventry
English Premier	22-02-1997	Nottm Forest	0-0	**Aston Villa**
English Premier	02-03-1997	**Aston Villa**	1-0	Liverpool
English Premier	05-03-1997	Leicester	1-0	**Aston Villa**
English Premier	15-03-1997	**Aston Villa**	0-0	West Ham
English Premier	22-03-1997	Blackburn	0-2	**Aston Villa**
English Premier	05-04-1997	**Aston Villa**	3-1	Everton
English Premier	09-04-1997	Wimbledon	0-2	**Aston Villa**
English Premier	12-04-1997	Derby	2-1	**Aston Villa**
English Premier	19-04-1997	**Aston Villa**	1-1	Tottenham
English Premier	22-04-1997	Leeds	0-0	**Aston Villa**
English Premier	03-05-1997	Middlesbro	3-2	**Aston Villa**
English Premier	11-05-1997	**Aston Villa**	1-0	Southampton

THE VILLA PREMIER YEARS - 1992-2010

Pos	Club	P	W	D	L	F	A	GD	Pts
1.	Manchester United	38	21	12	5	76	44	32	75
2.	Newcastle United	38	19	11	8	73	40	33	68
3.	Arsenal	38	19	11	8	62	32	30	68
4.	Liverpool	38	19	11	8	62	37	25	68
5.	Aston Villa	38	17	10	11	47	34	13	61
6.	Chelsea	38	16	11	11	58	55	3	59
7.	Sheffield Wednesday	38	14	15	9	50	51	-1	57
8.	Wimbledon	38	15	11	12	49	46	3	56
9.	Leicester City	38	12	11	15	46	54	-8	47
10.	Tottenham Hotspur	38	13	7	18	44	51	-7	46
11.	Leeds United	38	11	13	14	28	38	-10	46
12.	Derby County	38	11	13	14	45	58	-13	46
13.	Blackburn Rovers	38	9	15	14	42	43	-1	42
14.	Middlesbrough	38	10	12	16	51	60	-9	42
15.	West Ham United	38	10	12	16	39	48	-9	42
16.	Everton	38	10	12	16	44	57	-13	42
17.	Southampton	38	10	11	17	50	56	-6	41
18.	Coventry City	38	9	14	15	38	54	-16	41
19.	Sunderland	38	10	10	18	35	53	-18	40
20.	Nottingham Forest	38	6	16	16	31	59	-28	34

1996/97

Total
Played	**Won**	**Drawn**	**Lost**	**points**
38	17 (45 %)	10 (26 %)	11 (29 %)	61

Home
Played	**Won**	**Drawn**	**Lost**	**points**
19	11 (58 %)	5 (26 %)	3 (16 %)	38

Away
Played	**Won**	**Drawn**	**Lost**	**points**
19	6 (32 %)	5 (26 %)	8 (42 %)	23

THE VILLA PREMIER YEARS - 1992-2010

Biggest home win
Dec 22nd 1996   Aston Villa   5-0   Wimbledon

Biggest home loss
Nov 16th 1996   Aston Villa   1-3   Leicester City
Dec 26th 1996   Aston Villa   0-2   Chelsea

Biggest away win
Dec 4th 1996   West Ham Utd   0-2   Aston Villa
Mar 22nd 1997   Blackburn R.   0-2   Aston Villa
Apr 9th 1997   Wimbledon   0-2   Aston Villa

Biggest away loss
Jan 18th 1997   Liverpool   3-0   Aston Villa

Highest aggregate score home
Dec 22nd 1996   Aston Villa   5-0   Wimbledon

Highest aggregate score away
Sep 30th 1996   Newcastle Utd   4-3   Aston Villa

ASTON VILLA 1997/1998 RESULTS AND FIXTURES

English Premier	09-08-1997	Leicester	1-0	**Aston Villa**
English Premier	13-08-1997	**Aston Villa**	0-4	Blackburn
English Premier	23-08-1997	Newcastle	1-0	**Aston Villa**
English Premier	27-08-1997	Tottenham	3-2	**Aston Villa**
English Premier	30-08-1997	**Aston Villa**	1-0	Leeds
English Premier	13-09-1997	Barnsley	0-3	**Aston Villa**
English Premier	20-09-1997	**Aston Villa**	2-1	Derby
English Premier	22-09-1997	Liverpool	3-0	**Aston Villa**
English Premier	27-09-1997	**Aston Villa**	2-2	Sheff Wed
English Premier	04-10-1997	Bolton	0-1	**Aston Villa**
English Premier	18-10-1997	**Aston Villa**	1-2	Wimbledon
English Premier	26-10-1997	Arsenal	0-0	**Aston Villa**
English Premier	01-11-1997	**Aston Villa**	0-2	Chelsea
English Premier	08-11-1997	C Palace	1-1	**Aston Villa**
English Premier	22-11-1997	**Aston Villa**	2-1	Everton
English Premier	29-11-1997	West Ham	2-1	**Aston Villa**
English Premier	06-12-1997	**Aston Villa**	3-0	Coventry
English Premier	15-12-1997	Man Utd	1-0	**Aston Villa**
English Premier	20-12-1997	**Aston Villa**	1-1	Southampton
English Premier	26-12-1997	**Aston Villa**	4-1	Tottenham
English Premier	28-12-1997	Leeds	1-1	**Aston Villa**
English Premier	10-01-1998	**Aston Villa**	1-1	Leicester
English Premier	17-01-1998	Blackburn	5-0	**Aston Villa**
English Premier	01-02-1998	**Aston Villa**	0-1	Newcastle
English Premier	07-02-1998	Derby	0-1	**Aston Villa**
English Premier	18-02-1998	**Aston Villa**	0-2	Man Utd
English Premier	21-02-1998	Wimbledon	2-1	**Aston Villa**
English Premier	28-02-1998	**Aston Villa**	2-1	Liverpool
English Premier	08-03-1998	Chelsea	0-1	**Aston Villa**
English Premier	11-03-1998	**Aston Villa**	0-1	Barnsley
English Premier	14-03-1998	**Aston Villa**	3-1	C Palace
English Premier	28-03-1998	Everton	1-4	**Aston Villa**
English Premier	04-04-1998	**Aston Villa**	2-0	West Ham
English Premier	11-04-1998	Coventry	1-2	**Aston Villa**
English Premier	18-04-1998	Southampton	1-2	**Aston Villa**
English Premier	25-04-1998	**Aston Villa**	1-3	Bolton
English Premier	02-05-1998	Sheff Wed	1-3	**Aston Villa**
English Premier	10-05-1998	**Aston Villa**	1-0	Arsenal

THE VILLA PREMIER YEARS - 1992-2010

Pos	Club	P	W	D	L	F	A	GD	Pts
1.	Arsenal	38	23	9	6	68	33	35	78
2.	Manchester United	38	23	8	7	73	26	47	77
3.	Liverpool	38	18	11	9	68	42	26	65
4.	Chelsea	38	20	3	15	71	43	28	63
5.	Leeds United	38	17	8	13	57	46	11	59
6.	Blackburn Rovers	38	16	10	12	57	52	5	58
7.	**Aston Villa**	38	17	6	15	49	48	1	57
8.	West Ham United	38	16	8	14	56	57	-1	56
9.	Derby County	38	16	7	15	52	49	3	55
10.	Leicester City	38	13	14	11	51	41	10	53
11.	Coventry City	38	12	16	10	46	44	2	52
12.	Southampton	38	14	6	18	50	55	-5	48
13.	Newcastle United	38	11	11	16	35	44	-9	44
14.	Tottenham Hotspur	38	11	11	16	44	56	-12	44
15.	Wimbledon	38	10	14	14	34	46	-12	44
16.	Sheffield Wednesday	38	12	8	18	52	67	-15	44
17.	Everton	38	9	13	16	41	56	-15	40
18.	Bolton Wanderers	38	9	13	16	41	61	-20	40
19.	Barnsley	38	10	5	23	37	82	-45	35
20.	Crystal Palace	38	8	9	21	37	71	-34	33

Total
Played	Won	Drawn	Lost	points
38	17 (45 %)	6 (16 %)	15 (39 %)	57

Home
Played	Won	Drawn	Lost	points
19	9 (47 %)	3 (16 %)	7 (37 %)	30

Away
Played	Won	Drawn	Lost	points
19	8 (42 %)	3 (16 %)	8 (42 %)	27

Biggest home win
Dec 6th 1997	Aston Villa	3-0	Coventry City
Dec 26th 1997	Aston Villa	4-1	Tottenham H.

Biggest home loss
Aug 13th 1997	Aston Villa	0-4	Blackburn R.

Biggest away win
Sep 13th 1997	Barnsley	0-3	Aston Villa
Mar 28th 1998	Everton	1-4	Aston Villa

Biggest away loss
Jan 17th 1998	Blackburn Rovers	5-0	Aston Villa

Highest aggregate score home
Dec 26th 1997	Aston Villa	4-1	Tottenham H.

Highest aggregate score away
Aug 27th 1997	Tottenham H.	3-2	Aston Villa
Jan 17th 1998	Blackburn Rovers	5-0	Aston Villa
Mar 28th 1998	Everton	1-4	Aston Villa

ASTON VILLA 1998/1999 RESULTS AND FIXTURES

English Premier	15-08-1998	Everton	0-0	**Aston Villa**
English Premier	23-08-1998	**Aston Villa**	3-1	Middlesbro
English Premier	29-08-1998	Sheff Wed	0-1	**Aston Villa**
English Premier	09-09-1998	**Aston Villa**	1-0	Newcastle
English Premier	12-09-1998	**Aston Villa**	2-0	Wimbledon
English Premier	19-09-1998	Leeds	0-0	**Aston Villa**
English Premier	26-09-1998	**Aston Villa**	1-0	Derby
English Premier	03-10-1998	Coventry	1-2	**Aston Villa**
English Premier	17-10-1998	West Ham	0-0	**Aston Villa**
English Premier	24-10-1998	**Aston Villa**	1-1	Leicester
English Premier	07-11-1998	**Aston Villa**	3-2	Tottenham
English Premier	14-11-1998	Southampton	1-4	**Aston Villa**
English Premier	21-11-1998	**Aston Villa**	2-4	Liverpool
English Premier	28-11-1998	Nottm Forest	2-2	**Aston Villa**
English Premier	05-12-1998	**Aston Villa**	1-1	Man Utd
English Premier	09-12-1998	Chelsea	2-1	**Aston Villa**
English Premier	13-12-1998	**Aston Villa**	3-2	Arsenal
English Premier	21-12-1998	Charlton	0-1	**Aston Villa**
English Premier	26-12-1998	Blackburn	2-1	**Aston Villa**
English Premier	28-12-1998	**Aston Villa**	2-1	Sheff Wed
English Premier	09-01-1999	Middlesbro	0-0	**Aston Villa**
English Premier	18-01-1999	**Aston Villa**	3-0	Everton
English Premier	30-01-1999	Newcastle	2-1	**Aston Villa**
English Premier	06-02-1999	**Aston Villa**	1-3	Blackburn
English Premier	17-02-1999	**Aston Villa**	1-2	Leeds
English Premier	21-02-1999	Wimbledon	0-0	**Aston Villa**
English Premier	27-02-1999	**Aston Villa**	1-4	Coventry
English Premier	10-03-1999	Derby	2-1	**Aston Villa**
English Premier	13-03-1999	Tottenham	1-0	**Aston Villa**
English Premier	21-03-1999	**Aston Villa**	0-3	Chelsea
English Premier	02-04-1999	**Aston Villa**	0-0	West Ham
English Premier	06-04-1999	Leicester	2-2	**Aston Villa**
English Premier	10-04-1999	**Aston Villa**	3-0	Southampton
English Premier	17-04-1999	Liverpool	0-1	**Aston Villa**
English Premier	24-04-1999	**Aston Villa**	2-0	Nottm Forest
English Premier	01-05-1999	Man Utd	2-1	**Aston Villa**
English Premier	08-05-1999	**Aston Villa**	3-4	Charlton
English Premier	16-05-1999	Arsenal	1-0	**Aston Villa**

Pos	Club	P	W	D	L	F	A	GD	Pts
1.	Manchester United	38	22	13	3	80	37	43	79
2.	Arsenal	38	22	12	4	59	17	42	78
3.	Chelsea	38	20	15	3	57	30	27	75
4.	Leeds United	38	18	13	7	62	34	28	67
5.	West Ham United	38	16	9	13	46	53	-7	57
6.	**Aston Villa**	**38**	**15**	**10**	**13**	**51**	**46**	**5**	**55**
7.	Liverpool	38	15	9	14	68	49	19	54
8.	Derby County	38	13	13	12	40	45	-5	52
9.	Middlesbrough	38	12	15	11	48	54	-6	51
10.	Leicester City	38	12	13	13	40	46	-6	49
11.	Tottenham Hotspur	38	11	14	13	47	50	-3	47
12.	Sheffield Wednesday	38	13	7	18	41	42	-1	46
13.	Newcastle United	38	11	13	14	48	54	-6	46
14.	Everton	38	11	10	17	42	47	-5	43
15.	Coventry City	38	11	9	18	39	51	-12	42
16.	Wimbledon	38	10	12	16	40	63	-23	42
17.	Southampton	38	11	8	19	37	64	-27	41
18.	Charlton Athletic	38	8	12	18	41	56	-15	36
19.	Blackburn Rovers	38	7	14	17	38	52	-14	35
20.	Nottingham Forest	38	7	9	22	35	69	-34	30

1998/99

Total
Played	Won	Drawn	Lost	points
38	15 (39 %)	10 (26 %)	13 (34 %)	55

Home
Played	Won	Drawn	Lost	points
19	10 (53 %)	3 (16 %)	6 (32 %)	33

Away
Played	Won	Drawn	Lost	points
19	5 (26 %)	7 (37 %)	7 (37 %)	22

Biggest home win
Jan 18th 1999	Aston Villa	3-0	Everton
Apr 10th 1999	Aston Villa	3-0	Southampton

Biggest home loss
Feb 27th 1999	Aston Villa	1-4	Coventry City
Mar 21st 1999	Aston Villa	0-3	Chelsea

Biggest away win
Nov 14th 1998	Southampton	1-4	Aston Villa

Biggest away loss
Dec 9th 1998	Chelsea	2-1	Aston Villa
Dec 26th 1998	Blackburn R.	2-1	Aston Villa
Jan 30th 1999	Newcastle Utd	2-1	Aston Villa
Mar 10th 1999	Derby County	2-1	Aston Villa
Mar 13th 1999	Tottenham H.	1-0	Aston Villa
May 1st 1999	Manchester Utd	2-1	Aston Villa
May 16th 1999	Arsenal	1-0	Aston Villa

Highest aggregate score home
May 8th 1999	Aston Villa	3-4	Charlton Athletic

Highest aggregate score away
Nov 14th 1998	Southampton	1-4	Aston Villa

ASTON VILLA 1999/2000 RESULTS AND FIXTURES

League	Date	Home	Score	Away
English Premier	07-08-1999	Newcastle	0-1	**Aston Villa**
English Premier	11-08-1999	**Aston Villa**	3-0	Everton
English Premier	16-08-1999	**Aston Villa**	2-2	West Ham
English Premier	21-08-1999	Chelsea	1-0	**Aston Villa**
English Premier	24-08-1999	Watford	0-1	**Aston Villa**
English Premier	28-08-1999	**Aston Villa**	1-0	Middlesbro
English Premier	11-09-1999	Arsenal	3-1	**Aston Villa**
English Premier	18-09-1999	**Aston Villa**	1-0	Bradford
English Premier	25-09-1999	Leicester	3-1	**Aston Villa**
English Premier	02-10-1999	**Aston Villa**	0-0	Liverpool
English Premier	18-10-1999	Sunderland	2-1	**Aston Villa**
English Premier	23-10-1999	**Aston Villa**	1-1	Wimbledon
English Premier	30-10-1999	Man Utd	3-0	**Aston Villa**
English Premier	06-11-1999	**Aston Villa**	0-1	Southampton
English Premier	22-11-1999	Coventry	2-1	**Aston Villa**
English Premier	27-11-1999	Everton	0-0	**Aston Villa**
English Premier	04-12-1999	**Aston Villa**	0-1	Newcastle
English Premier	18-12-1999	**Aston Villa**	2-1	Sheff Wed
English Premier	26-12-1999	Derby	0-2	**Aston Villa**
English Premier	29-12-1999	**Aston Villa**	1-1	Tottenham
English Premier	03-01-2000	Leeds	1-2	**Aston Villa**
English Premier	15-01-2000	West Ham	1-1	**Aston Villa**
English Premier	22-01-2000	**Aston Villa**	0-0	Chelsea
English Premier	05-02-2000	**Aston Villa**	4-0	Watford
English Premier	14-02-2000	Middlesbro	0-4	**Aston Villa**
English Premier	26-02-2000	Bradford	1-1	**Aston Villa**
English Premier	05-03-2000	**Aston Villa**	1-1	Arsenal
English Premier	11-03-2000	**Aston Villa**	1-0	Coventry
English Premier	15-03-2000	Liverpool	0-0	**Aston Villa**
English Premier	18-03-2000	Southampton	2-0	**Aston Villa**
English Premier	25-03-2000	**Aston Villa**	2-0	Derby
English Premier	05-04-2000	Sheff Wed	0-1	**Aston Villa**
English Premier	09-04-2000	**Aston Villa**	1-0	Leeds
English Premier	15-04-2000	Tottenham	2-4	**Aston Villa**
English Premier	22-04-2000	**Aston Villa**	2-2	Leicester
English Premier	29-04-2000	**Aston Villa**	1-1	Sunderland
English Premier	06-05-2000	Wimbledon	2-2	**Aston Villa**
English Premier	14-05-2000	**Aston Villa**	0-1	Man Utd

THE VILLA PREMIER YEARS - 1992-2010

Pos	Club	P	W	D	L	F	A	GD	Pts
1.	Manchester United	38	28	7	3	97	45	52	91
2.	Arsenal	38	22	7	9	73	43	30	73
3.	Leeds United	38	21	6	11	58	43	15	69
4.	Liverpool	38	19	10	9	51	30	21	67
5.	Chelsea	38	18	11	9	53	34	19	65
6.	Aston Villa	38	15	13	10	46	35	11	58
7.	Sunderland	38	16	10	12	57	56	1	58
8.	Leicester City	38	16	7	15	55	55	0	55
9.	West Ham United	38	15	10	13	52	53	-1	55
10.	Tottenham Hotspur	38	15	8	15	57	49	8	53
11.	Newcastle United	38	14	10	14	63	54	9	52
12.	Middlesbrough	38	14	10	14	46	52	-6	52
13.	Everton	38	12	14	12	59	49	10	50
14.	Coventry City	38	12	8	18	47	54	-7	44
15.	Southampton	38	12	8	18	45	62	-17	44
16.	Derby County	38	9	11	18	44	57	-13	38
17.	Bradford City	38	9	9	20	38	68	-30	36
18.	Wimbledon	38	7	12	19	46	74	-28	33
19.	Sheffield Wednesday	38	8	7	23	38	70	-32	31
20.	Watford	38	6	6	26	35	77	-42	24

Total
Played	Won	Drawn	Lost	points
38	15 (39 %)	13 (34 %)	10 (26 %)	58

Home
Played	Won	Drawn	Lost	points
19	8 (42 %)	8 (42 %)	3 (16 %)	32

Away
Played	Won	Drawn	Lost	points
19	7 (37 %)	5 (26 %)	7 (37 %)	26

THE VILLA PREMIER YEARS - 1992-2010

Biggest home win
Feb 5th 2000   Aston Villa   4-0   Watford

Biggest home loss
Nov 6th 1999   Aston Villa   0-1   Southampton
Dec 4th 1999   Aston Villa   0-1   Newcastle United
May 14th 2000 Aston Villa   0-1   Manchester Utd

Biggest away win
Feb 14th 2000 Middlesbrough   0-4   Aston Villa

Biggest away loss
Oct 30th 1999 Manchester Utd   3-0   Aston Villa

Highest aggregate score home
Aug 16th 1999 Aston Villa   2-2   West Ham
Feb 5th 2000   Aston Villa   4-0   Watford
Apr 22nd 2000 Aston Villa   2-2   Leicester City

Highest aggregate score away
Apr 15th 2000 Tottenham H.   2-4   Aston Villa

ASTON VILLA 2000/01 RESULTS AND FIXTURES

English Premier	19-08-2000	Leicester	0-0	**Aston Villa**
English Premier	27-08-2000	**Aston Villa**	1-1	Chelsea
English Premier	06-09-2000	Liverpool	3-1	**Aston Villa**
English Premier	09-09-2000	Ipswich	1-2	**Aston Villa**
English Premier	16-09-2000	**Aston Villa**	2-0	Bradford
English Premier	23-09-2000	Middlesbro	1-1	**Aston Villa**
English Premier	30-09-2000	**Aston Villa**	4-1	Derby
English Premier	14-10-2000	Arsenal	1-0	**Aston Villa**
English Premier	22-10-2000	**Aston Villa**	0-0	Sunderland
English Premier	28-10-2000	**Aston Villa**	2-1	Charlton
English Premier	05-11-2000	Everton	0-1	**Aston Villa**
English Premier	11-11-2000	**Aston Villa**	2-0	Tottenham
English Premier	18-11-2000	Southampton	2-0	**Aston Villa**
English Premier	25-11-2000	Coventry	1-1	**Aston Villa**
English Premier	02-12-2000	**Aston Villa**	1-1	Newcastle
English Premier	09-12-2000	West Ham	1-1	**Aston Villa**
English Premier	16-12-2000	**Aston Villa**	2-2	Man City
English Premier	23-12-2000	Leeds	1-2	**Aston Villa**
English Premier	26-12-2000	**Aston Villa**	0-1	Man Utd
English Premier	01-01-2001	Chelsea	1-0	**Aston Villa**
English Premier	13-01-2001	**Aston Villa**	0-3	Liverpool
English Premier	20-01-2001	Man Utd	2-0	**Aston Villa**
English Premier	24-01-2001	**Aston Villa**	1-2	Leeds
English Premier	03-02-2001	Bradford	0-3	**Aston Villa**
English Premier	10-02-2001	**Aston Villa**	1-1	Middlesbro
English Premier	24-02-2001	Derby	1-0	**Aston Villa**
English Premier	05-03-2001	Sunderland	1-1	**Aston Villa**
English Premier	10-03-2001	**Aston Villa**	2-1	Ipswich
English Premier	18-03-2001	**Aston Villa**	0-0	Arsenal
English Premier	31-03-2001	Man City	1-3	**Aston Villa**
English Premier	04-04-2001	**Aston Villa**	2-1	Leicester
English Premier	07-04-2001	**Aston Villa**	2-2	West Ham
English Premier	14-04-2001	**Aston Villa**	2-1	Everton
English Premier	17-04-2001	Charlton	3-3	**Aston Villa**
English Premier	21-04-2001	**Aston Villa**	0-0	Southampton
English Premier	28-04-2001	Tottenham	0-0	**Aston Villa**
English Premier	05-05-2001	**Aston Villa**	3-2	Coventry
English Premier	19-05-2001	Newcastle	3-0	**Aston Villa**

THE VILLA PREMIER YEARS - 1992-2010

Pos	Club	P	W	D	L	F	A	GD	Pts
1.	Manchester United	38	24	8	6	79	31	48	80
2.	Arsenal	38	20	10	8	63	38	25	70
3.	Liverpool	38	20	9	9	71	39	32	69
4.	Leeds United	38	20	8	10	64	43	21	68
5.	Ipswich Town	38	20	6	12	57	42	15	66
6.	Chelsea	38	17	10	11	68	45	23	61
7.	Sunderland	38	15	12	11	46	41	5	57
8.	Aston Villa	38	13	15	10	46	43	3	54
9.	Charlton Athletic	38	14	10	14	50	57	-7	52
10.	Southampton	38	14	10	14	40	48	-8	52
11.	Newcastle United	38	14	9	15	44	50	-6	51
12.	Tottenham Hotspur	38	13	10	15	47	54	-7	49
13.	Leicester City	38	14	6	18	39	51	-12	48
14.	Middlesbrough	38	9	15	14	44	44	0	42
15.	West Ham United	38	10	12	16	45	50	-5	42
16.	Everton	38	11	9	18	45	59	-14	42
17.	Derby County	38	10	12	16	37	59	-22	42
18.	Manchester City	38	8	10	20	41	65	-24	34
19.	Coventry City	38	8	10	20	36	63	-27	34
20.	Bradford City	38	5	11	22	30	70	-40	26

2000/01

Total
Played	Won	Drawn	Lost	points
38	13 (34 %)	15 (39 %)	10 (26 %)	54

Home
Played	Won	Drawn	Lost	points
19	8 (42 %)	8 (42 %)	3 (16 %)	32

Away
Played	Won	Drawn	Lost	points
19	5 (26 %)	7 (37 %)	7 (37 %)	22

THE VILLA PREMIER YEARS - 1992-2010

Biggest home win
Sep 30th 2000 Aston Villa   4-1   Derby County

Biggest home loss
Jan 13th 2001 Aston Villa   0-3   Liverpool

Biggest away win
Feb 3rd 2001   Bradford City   0-3   Aston Villa

Biggest away loss
May 19th 2001 Newcastle United   3-0   Aston Villa

Highest aggregate score home
Sep 30th 2000 Aston Villa   4-1   Derby County
May 5th 2001   Aston Villa   3-2   Coventry City

Highest aggregate score away
Apr 17th 2001 Charlton Athletic   3-3   Aston Villa

ASTON VILLA 2001/02 RESULTS AND FIXTURES

English Premier	18-08-2001	Tottenham	0-0	**Aston Villa**
English Premier	26-08-2001	**Aston Villa**	1-1	Man Utd
English Premier	08-09-2001	Liverpool	1-3	**Aston Villa**
English Premier	16-09-2001	**Aston Villa**	0-0	Sunderland
English Premier	24-09-2001	Southampton	1-3	**Aston Villa**
English Premier	30-09-2001	**Aston Villa**	2-0	Blackburn
English Premier	14-10-2001	**Aston Villa**	2-0	Fulham
English Premier	20-10-2001	Everton	3-2	**Aston Villa**
English Premier	24-10-2001	**Aston Villa**	1-0	Charlton
English Premier	27-10-2001	**Aston Villa**	3-2	Bolton
English Premier	03-11-2001	Newcastle	3-0	**Aston Villa**
English Premier	17-11-2001	**Aston Villa**	0-0	Middlesbro
English Premier	25-11-2001	Leeds	1-1	**Aston Villa**
English Premier	01-12-2001	**Aston Villa**	0-2	Leicester
English Premier	05-12-2001	West Ham	1-1	**Aston Villa**
English Premier	09-12-2001	Arsenal	3-2	**Aston Villa**
English Premier	17-12-2001	**Aston Villa**	2-1	Ipswich
English Premier	22-12-2001	Derby	3-1	**Aston Villa**
English Premier	26-12-2001	**Aston Villa**	1-2	Liverpool
English Premier	29-12-2001	**Aston Villa**	1-1	Tottenham
English Premier	01-01-2002	Sunderland	1-1	**Aston Villa**
English Premier	12-01-2002	**Aston Villa**	2-1	Derby
English Premier	21-01-2002	Charlton	1-2	**Aston Villa**
English Premier	30-01-2002	**Aston Villa**	0-0	Everton
English Premier	02-02-2002	Fulham	0-0	**Aston Villa**
English Premier	09-02-2002	**Aston Villa**	1-1	Chelsea
English Premier	23-02-2002	Man Utd	1-0	**Aston Villa**
English Premier	02-03-2002	**Aston Villa**	2-1	West Ham
English Premier	05-03-2002	Blackburn	3-0	**Aston Villa**
English Premier	17-03-2002	**Aston Villa**	1-2	Arsenal
English Premier	23-03-2002	Ipswich	0-0	**Aston Villa**
English Premier	30-03-2002	Bolton	3-2	**Aston Villa**
English Premier	02-04-2002	**Aston Villa**	1-1	Newcastle
English Premier	06-04-2002	Middlesbro	2-1	**Aston Villa**
English Premier	13-04-2002	**Aston Villa**	0-1	Leeds
English Premier	20-04-2002	Leicester	2-2	**Aston Villa**
English Premier	27-04-2002	**Aston Villa**	2-1	Southampton
English Premier	11-05-2002	Chelsea	1-3	**Aston Villa**

THE VILLA PREMIER YEARS - 1992-2010

Pos	Club	P	W	D	L	F	A	GD	Pts
1.	Arsenal	38	26	9	3	79	36	43	87
2.	Liverpool	38	24	8	6	67	30	37	80
3.	Manchester United	38	24	5	9	87	45	42	77
4.	Newcastle United	38	21	8	9	74	52	22	71
5.	Leeds United	38	18	12	8	53	37	16	66
6.	Chelsea	38	17	13	8	66	38	28	64
7.	West Ham United	38	15	8	15	48	57	-9	53
8.	**Aston Villa**	**38**	**12**	**14**	**12**	**46**	**47**	**-1**	**50**
9.	Tottenham Hotspur	38	14	8	16	49	53	-4	50
10.	Blackburn Rovers	38	12	10	16	55	51	4	46
11.	Southampton	38	12	9	17	46	54	-8	45
12.	Middlesbrough	38	12	9	17	35	47	-12	45
13.	Fulham	38	10	14	14	36	44	-8	44
14.	Charlton Athletic	38	10	14	14	38	49	-11	44
15.	Everton	38	11	10	17	45	57	-12	43
16.	Bolton Wanderers	38	9	13	16	44	62	-18	40
17.	Sunderland	38	10	10	18	29	51	-22	40
18.	Ipswich Town	38	9	9	20	41	64	-23	36
19.	Derby County	38	8	6	24	33	63	-30	30
20.	Leicester City	38	5	13	20	30	64	-34	28

Total
Played	Won	Drawn	Lost	points
38	12 (32 %)	14 (37 %)	12 (32 %)	50

Home
Played	Won	Drawn	Lost	points
19	8 (42 %)	7 (37 %)	4 (21 %)	31

Away
Played	Won	Drawn	Lost	points
19	4 (21 %)	7 (37 %)	8 (42 %)	19

Biggest home win
Sep 30th 2001   Aston Villa   2-0   Blackburn R.

Oct 14th 2001	Aston Villa	2-0	Fulham

Biggest home loss

Dec 1st 2001	Aston Villa	0-2	Leicester City

Biggest away win

Sep 8th 2001	Liverpool	1-3	Aston Villa
Sep 24th 2001	Southampton	1-3	Aston Villa
May 11th 2002	Chelsea	1-3	Aston Villa

Biggest away loss

Nov 3rd 2001	Newcastle Utd	3-0	Aston Villa
Mar 5th 2002	Blackburn Rovers	3-0	Aston Villa

Highest aggregate score home

Oct 27th 2001	Aston Villa	3-2	Bolton W.

Highest aggregate score away

Oct 20th 2001	Everton	3-2	Aston Villa
Dec 9th 2001	Arsenal	3-2	Aston Villa
Mar 30th 2002	Bolton W.	3-2	Aston Villa

ASTON VILLA 2002/03 RESULTS AND FIXTURES

Competition	Date	Home	Score	Away
English Premier	18-08-2002	**Aston Villa**	0-1	Liverpool
English Premier	24-08-2002	Tottenham	1-0	**Aston Villa**
English Premier	28-08-2002	**Aston Villa**	1-0	Man City
English Premier	01-09-2002	Bolton	1-0	**Aston Villa**
English Premier	11-09-2002	**Aston Villa**	2-0	Charlton
English Premier	16-09-2002	Birmingham	3-0	**Aston Villa**
English Premier	22-09-2002	**Aston Villa**	3-2	Everton
English Premier	28-09-2002	Sunderland	1-0	**Aston Villa**
English Premier	06-10-2002	**Aston Villa**	0-0	Leeds
English Premier	21-10-2002	**Aston Villa**	0-1	Southampton
English Premier	26-10-2002	Man Utd	1-1	**Aston Villa**
English Premier	03-11-2002	Blackburn	0-0	**Aston Villa**
English Premier	09-11-2002	**Aston Villa**	3-1	Fulham
English Premier	16-11-2002	West Brom	0-0	**Aston Villa**
English Premier	23-11-2002	**Aston Villa**	4-1	West Ham
English Premier	30-11-2002	Arsenal	3-1	**Aston Villa**
English Premier	07-12-2002	**Aston Villa**	0-1	Newcastle
English Premier	14-12-2002	**Aston Villa**	2-1	West Brom
English Premier	21-12-2002	Chelsea	2-0	**Aston Villa**
English Premier	26-12-2002	Man City	3-1	**Aston Villa**
English Premier	28-12-2002	**Aston Villa**	1-0	Middlesbro
English Premier	01-01-2003	**Aston Villa**	2-0	Bolton
English Premier	11-01-2003	Liverpool	1-1	**Aston Villa**
English Premier	18-01-2003	**Aston Villa**	0-1	Tottenham
English Premier	28-01-2003	Middlesbro	2-5	**Aston Villa**
English Premier	02-02-2003	**Aston Villa**	3-0	Blackburn
English Premier	08-02-2003	Fulham	2-1	**Aston Villa**
English Premier	22-02-2003	Charlton	3-0	**Aston Villa**
English Premier	03-03-2003	**Aston Villa**	0-2	Birmingham
English Premier	15-03-2003	**Aston Villa**	0-1	Man Utd
English Premier	22-03-2003	Southampton	2-2	**Aston Villa**
English Premier	05-04-2003	**Aston Villa**	1-1	Arsenal
English Premier	12-04-2003	West Ham	2-2	**Aston Villa**
English Premier	19-04-2003	**Aston Villa**	2-1	Chelsea
English Premier	21-04-2003	Newcastle	1-1	**Aston Villa**
English Premier	26-04-2003	Everton	2-1	**Aston Villa**
English Premier	03-05-2003	**Aston Villa**	1-0	Sunderland
English Premier	11-05-2003	Leeds	3-1	**Aston Villa**

THE VILLA PREMIER YEARS - 1992-2010

Pos	Club	P	W	D	L	F	A	GD	Pts
1.	Manchester United	38	25	8	5	74	34	40	83
2.	Arsenal	38	23	9	6	85	42	43	78
3.	Newcastle United	38	21	6	11	63	48	15	69
4.	Chelsea	38	19	10	9	68	38	30	67
5.	Liverpool	38	18	10	10	61	41	20	64
6.	Blackburn Rovers	38	16	12	10	52	43	9	60
7.	Everton	38	17	8	13	48	48	0	59
8.	Southampton	38	13	13	12	43	46	-3	52
9.	Manchester City	38	15	6	17	47	54	-7	51
10.	Tottenham Hotspur	38	14	8	16	51	62	-11	50
11.	Middlesbrough	38	13	10	15	48	44	4	49
12.	Charlton Athletic	38	14	7	17	45	56	-11	49
13.	Birmingham City	38	13	9	16	41	49	-8	48
14.	Fulham	38	13	9	16	41	50	-9	48
15.	Leeds United	38	14	5	19	58	57	1	47
16.	Aston Villa	38	12	9	17	42	47	-5	45
17.	Bolton Wanderers	38	10	14	14	40	51	-11	44
18.	West Ham United	38	10	12	16	42	59	-17	42
19.	West Bromwich Albion	38	6	8	24	29	65	-36	26
20.	Sunderland	38	4	7	27	21	65	-44	19

2002/03

Total
Played	Won	Drawn	Lost	points
38	12 (32 %)	9 (24 %)	17 (45 %)	45

Home
Played	Won	Drawn	Lost	points
19	11 (58 %)	2 (11 %)	6 (32 %)	35

Away
Played	Won	Drawn	Lost	points
19	1 (5 %)	7 (37 %)	11 (58 %)	10

THE VILLA PREMIER YEARS - 1992-2010

Biggest home win
Nov 23rd 2002	Aston Villa	4-1	West Ham
Feb 2nd 2003	Aston Villa	3-0	Blackburn Rovers

Biggest home loss
Mar 3rd 2003	Aston Villa	0-2	Birmingham City

Biggest away win
Jan 28th 2003	Middlesbrough	2-5	Aston Villa

Biggest away loss
Sep 16th 2002	Birmingham City	3-0	Aston Villa
Feb 22nd 2003	Charlton Athletic	3-0	Aston Villa

Highest aggregate score home
Sep 22nd 2002	Aston Villa	3-2	Everton
Nov 23rd 2002	Aston Villa	4-1	West Ham United

Highest aggregate score away
Jan 28th 2003	Middlesbrough	2-5	Aston Villa

ASTON VILLA 2003/04 RESULTS AND FIXTURES

English Premier	16-08-2003	Portsmouth	2-1	**Aston Villa**
English Premier	24-08-2003	**Aston Villa**	0-0	Liverpool
English Premier	27-08-2003	Arsenal	2-0	**Aston Villa**
English Premier	30-08-2003	**Aston Villa**	3-1	Leicester
English Premier	14-09-2003	Man City	4-1	**Aston Villa**
English Premier	20-09-2003	**Aston Villa**	2-1	Charlton
English Premier	27-09-2003	Chelsea	1-0	**Aston Villa**
English Premier	05-10-2003	**Aston Villa**	1-1	Bolton
English Premier	19-10-2003	Birmingham	0-0	**Aston Villa**
English Premier	25-10-2003	**Aston Villa**	0-0	Everton
English Premier	01-11-2003	Newcastle	1-1	**Aston Villa**
English Premier	08-11-2003	**Aston Villa**	0-2	Middlesbro
English Premier	23-11-2003	Tottenham	2-1	**Aston Villa**
English Premier	29-11-2003	**Aston Villa**	1-0	Southampton
English Premier	06-12-2003	Man Utd	4-0	**Aston Villa**
English Premier	14-12-2003	**Aston Villa**	3-2	Wolves
English Premier	20-12-2003	Blackburn	0-2	**Aston Villa**
English Premier	26-12-2003	Leeds	0-0	**Aston Villa**
English Premier	28-12-2003	**Aston Villa**	3-0	Fulham
English Premier	06-01-2004	**Aston Villa**	2-1	Portsmouth
English Premier	10-01-2004	Liverpool	1-0	**Aston Villa**
English Premier	18-01-2004	**Aston Villa**	0-2	Arsenal
English Premier	31-01-2004	Leicester	0-5	**Aston Villa**
English Premier	07-02-2004	**Aston Villa**	2-0	Leeds
English Premier	11-02-2004	Fulham	1-2	**Aston Villa**
English Premier	22-02-2004	**Aston Villa**	2-2	Birmingham
English Premier	28-02-2004	Everton	2-0	**Aston Villa**
English Premier	14-03-2004	Wolves	0-4	**Aston Villa**
English Premier	20-03-2004	**Aston Villa**	0-2	Blackburn
English Premier	27-03-2004	Charlton	1-2	**Aston Villa**
English Premier	04-04-2004	**Aston Villa**	1-1	Man City
English Premier	10-04-2004	Bolton	2-2	**Aston Villa**
English Premier	12-04-2004	**Aston Villa**	3-2	Chelsea
English Premier	18-04-2004	**Aston Villa**	0-0	Newcastle
English Premier	24-04-2004	Middlesbro	1-2	**Aston Villa**
English Premier	02-05-2004	**Aston Villa**	1-0	Tottenham
English Premier	08-05-2004	Southampton	1-1	**Aston Villa**
English Premier	15-05-2004	**Aston Villa**	0-2	Man Utd

THE VILLA PREMIER YEARS - 1992-2010

Pos	Club	P	W	D	L	F	A	GD	Pts
1.	Arsenal	38	26	12	0	73	26	47	90
2.	Chelsea	38	24	7	7	67	30	37	79
3.	Manchester United	38	23	6	9	64	35	29	75
4.	Liverpool	38	16	12	10	55	37	18	60
5.	Newcastle United	38	13	17	8	52	40	12	56
6.	Aston Villa	38	15	11	12	48	44	4	56
7.	Charlton Athletic	38	14	11	13	51	51	0	53
8.	Bolton Wanderers	38	14	11	13	48	56	-8	53
9.	Fulham	38	14	10	14	52	46	6	52
10.	Birmingham City	38	12	14	12	43	48	-5	50
11.	Middlesbrough	38	13	9	16	44	52	-8	48
12.	Southampton	38	12	11	15	44	45	-1	47
13.	Portsmouth	38	12	9	17	47	54	-7	45
14.	Tottenham Hotspur	38	13	6	19	47	57	-10	45
15.	Blackburn Rovers	38	12	8	18	51	59	-8	44
16.	Manchester City	38	9	14	15	55	54	1	41
17.	Everton	38	9	12	17	45	57	-12	39
18.	Leicester City	38	6	15	17	48	65	-17	33
19.	Leeds United	38	8	9	21	40	79	-39	33
20.	Wolverhampton W.	38	7	12	19	38	77	-39	33

Total
Played	Won	Drawn	Lost	points
38	15 (39 %)	11 (29 %)	12 (32 %)	56

Home
Played	Won	Drawn	Lost	points
19	9 (47 %)	6 (32 %)	4 (21 %)	33

Away
Played	Won	Drawn	Lost	points
19	6 (32 %)	5 (26 %)	8 (42 %)	23

Biggest home win
Dec 28th 2003 Aston Villa 3-0 Fulham

Biggest home loss
Nov 8th 2003 Aston Villa 0-2 Middlesbrough
Jan 18th 2004 Aston Villa 0-2 Arsenal
Mar 20th 2004 Aston Villa 0-2 Blackburn Rovers
May 15th 2004 Aston Villa 0-2 Manchester Utd

Biggest away win
Jan 31st 2004 Leicester City 0-5 Aston Villa

Biggest away loss
Dec 6th 2003 Manchester Utd 4-0 Aston Villa

Highest aggregate score home
Dec 14th 2003 Aston Villa 3-2 Wolves
Apr 12th 2004 Aston Villa 3-2 Chelsea

Highest aggregate score away
Sep 14th 2003 Manchester City 4-1 Aston Villa
Jan 31st 2004 Leicester City 0-5 Aston Villa

ASTON VILLA 2004/05 RESULTS AND FIXTURES

English Premier	14-08-2004	**Aston Villa**	2-0	Southampton
English Premier	22-08-2004	West Brom	1-1	**Aston Villa**
English Premier	25-08-2004	Charlton	3-0	**Aston Villa**
English Premier	28-08-2004	**Aston Villa**	4-2	Newcastle
English Premier	11-09-2004	**Aston Villa**	0-0	Chelsea
English Premier	18-09-2004	Norwich	0-0	**Aston Villa**
English Premier	25-09-2004	**Aston Villa**	1-1	C Palace
English Premier	02-10-2004	Blackburn	2-2	**Aston Villa**
English Premier	16-10-2004	Arsenal	3-1	**Aston Villa**
English Premier	23-10-2004	**Aston Villa**	2-0	Fulham
English Premier	30-10-2004	Everton	1-1	**Aston Villa**
English Premier	06-11-2004	**Aston Villa**	3-0	Portsmouth
English Premier	13-11-2004	Bolton	1-2	**Aston Villa**
English Premier	22-11-2004	**Aston Villa**	1-0	Tottenham
English Premier	27-11-2004	Man City	2-0	**Aston Villa**
English Premier	04-12-2004	**Aston Villa**	1-1	Liverpool
English Premier	12-12-2004	**Aston Villa**	1-2	Birmingham
English Premier	18-12-2004	Middlesbro	3-0	**Aston Villa**
English Premier	26-12-2004	Chelsea	1-0	**Aston Villa**
English Premier	28-12-2004	**Aston Villa**	0-1	Man Utd
English Premier	01-01-2005	**Aston Villa**	1-0	Blackburn
English Premier	03-01-2005	C Palace	2-0	**Aston Villa**
English Premier	15-01-2005	**Aston Villa**	3-0	Norwich
English Premier	22-01-2005	Man Utd	3-1	**Aston Villa**
English Premier	02-02-2005	Fulham	1-1	**Aston Villa**
English Premier	05-02-2005	**Aston Villa**	1-3	Arsenal
English Premier	12-02-2005	Portsmouth	1-2	**Aston Villa**
English Premier	26-02-2005	**Aston Villa**	1-3	Everton
English Premier	05-03-2005	**Aston Villa**	2-0	Middlesbro
English Premier	20-03-2005	Birmingham	2-0	**Aston Villa**
English Premier	02-04-2005	Newcastle	0-3	**Aston Villa**
English Premier	10-04-2005	**Aston Villa**	1-1	West Brom
English Premier	16-04-2005	Southampton	2-3	**Aston Villa**
English Premier	20-04-2005	**Aston Villa**	0-0	Charlton
English Premier	23-04-2005	**Aston Villa**	1-1	Bolton
English Premier	01-05-2005	Tottenham	5-1	**Aston Villa**
English Premier	07-05-2005	**Aston Villa**	1-2	Man City
English Premier	15-05-2005	Liverpool	2-1	**Aston Villa**

THE VILLA PREMIER YEARS - 1992-2010

Pos	Club	P	W	D	L	F	A	GD	Pts
1.	Chelsea	38	29	8	1	72	15	57	95
2.	Arsenal	38	25	8	5	87	36	51	83
3.	Manchester United	38	22	11	5	58	26	32	77
4.	Everton	38	18	7	13	45	46	-1	61
5.	Liverpool	38	17	7	14	52	41	11	58
6.	Bolton Wanderers	38	16	10	12	49	44	5	58
7.	Middlesbrough	38	14	13	11	53	46	7	55
8.	Manchester City	38	13	13	12	47	39	8	52
9.	Tottenham Hotspur	38	14	10	14	47	41	6	52
10.	Aston Villa	38	12	11	15	45	52	-7	47
11.	Charlton Athletic	38	12	10	16	42	58	-16	46
12.	Birmingham City	38	11	12	15	40	46	-6	45
13.	Fulham	38	12	8	18	52	60	-8	44
14.	Newcastle United	38	10	14	14	47	57	-10	44
15.	Blackburn Rovers	38	9	15	14	32	43	-11	42
16.	Portsmouth	38	10	9	19	43	59	-16	39
17.	West Bromwich Albion	38	6	16	16	36	61	-25	34
18.	Crystal Palace	38	7	12	19	41	62	-21	33
19.	Norwich City	38	7	12	19	42	77	-35	33
20.	Southampton	38	6	14	18	45	66	-21	32

Total

Played	Won	Drawn	Lost	points
38	12 (32 %)	11 (29 %)	15 (39 %)	47

Home

Played	Won	Drawn	Lost	points
19	8 (42 %)	6 (32 %)	5 (26 %)	30

Away

Played	Won	Drawn	Lost	points
19	4 (21 %)	5 (26 %)	10 (53 %)	17

THE VILLA PREMIER YEARS - 1992-2010

Biggest home win
Nov 6th 2004   Aston Villa   3-0   Portsmouth
Jan 15th 2005 Aston Villa   3-0   Norwich City

Biggest home loss
Feb 5th 2005   Aston Villa   1-3   Arsenal
Feb 26th 2005 Aston Villa   1-3   Everton

Biggest away win
Apr 2nd 2005   Newcastle United   0-3   Aston Villa

Biggest away loss
May 1st 2005   Tottenham H.   5-1   Aston Villa

Highest aggregate score home
Aug 28th 2004 Aston Villa   4-2   Newcastle United

Highest aggregate score away
May 1st 2005   Tottenham H.   5-1   Aston Villa

ASTON VILLA 2005/06 RESULTS AND FIXTURES

English Premier	13-08-2005	**Aston Villa**	2-2	Bolton
English Premier	20-08-2005	Man Utd	1-0	**Aston Villa**
English Premier	23-08-2005	Portsmouth	1-1	**Aston Villa**
English Premier	27-08-2005	**Aston Villa**	1-0	Blackburn
English Premier	12-09-2005	West Ham	4-0	**Aston Villa**
English Premier	17-09-2005	**Aston Villa**	1-1	Tottenham
English Premier	24-09-2005	Chelsea	2-1	**Aston Villa**
English Premier	02-10-2005	**Aston Villa**	2-3	Middlesbro
English Premier	16-10-2005	Birmingham	0-1	**Aston Villa**
English Premier	22-10-2005	**Aston Villa**	0-2	Wigan
English Premier	31-10-2005	Man City	3-1	**Aston Villa**
English Premier	05-11-2005	**Aston Villa**	0-2	Liverpool
English Premier	19-11-2005	Sunderland	1-3	**Aston Villa**
English Premier	26-11-2005	**Aston Villa**	1-0	Charlton
English Premier	03-12-2005	Newcastle	1-1	**Aston Villa**
English Premier	10-12-2005	Bolton	1-1	**Aston Villa**
English Premier	17-12-2005	**Aston Villa**	0-2	Man Utd
English Premier	26-12-2005	**Aston Villa**	4-0	Everton
English Premier	28-12-2005	Fulham	3-3	**Aston Villa**
English Premier	31-12-2005	**Aston Villa**	0-0	Arsenal
English Premier	02-01-2006	West Brom	1-2	**Aston Villa**
English Premier	14-01-2006	**Aston Villa**	1-2	West Ham
English Premier	21-01-2006	Tottenham	0-0	**Aston Villa**
English Premier	01-02-2006	**Aston Villa**	1-1	Chelsea
English Premier	04-02-2006	Middlesbro	0-4	**Aston Villa**
English Premier	11-02-2006	**Aston Villa**	1-2	Newcastle
English Premier	25-02-2006	Charlton	0-0	**Aston Villa**
English Premier	04-03-2006	**Aston Villa**	1-0	Portsmouth
English Premier	11-03-2006	Blackburn	2-0	**Aston Villa**
English Premier	18-03-2006	Everton	4-1	**Aston Villa**
English Premier	25-03-2006	**Aston Villa**	0-0	Fulham
English Premier	01-04-2006	Arsenal	5-0	**Aston Villa**
English Premier	09-04-2006	**Aston Villa**	0-0	West Brom
English Premier	16-04-2006	**Aston Villa**	3-1	Birmingham
English Premier	18-04-2006	Wigan	3-2	**Aston Villa**
English Premier	25-04-2006	**Aston Villa**	0-1	Man City
English Premier	29-04-2006	Liverpool	3-1	**Aston Villa**
English Premier	07-05-2006	**Aston Villa**	2-1	Sunderland

THE VILLA PREMIER YEARS - 1992-2010

Pos	Club	P	W	D	L	F	A	GD	Pts
1.	Chelsea	38	29	4	5	72	22	50	91
2.	Manchester United	38	25	8	5	72	34	38	83
3.	Liverpool	38	25	7	6	57	25	32	82
4.	Arsenal	38	20	7	11	68	31	37	67
5.	Tottenham Hotspur	38	18	11	9	53	38	15	65
6.	Blackburn Rovers	38	19	6	13	51	42	9	63
7.	Newcastle United	38	17	7	14	47	42	5	58
8.	Bolton Wanderers	38	15	11	12	49	41	8	56
9.	West Ham United	38	16	7	15	52	55	-3	55
10.	Wigan Athletic	38	15	6	17	45	52	-7	51
11.	Everton	38	14	8	16	34	49	-15	50
12.	Fulham	38	14	6	18	48	58	-10	48
13.	Charlton Athletic	38	13	8	17	41	55	-14	47
14.	Middlesbrough	38	12	9	17	48	58	-10	45
15.	Manchester City	38	13	4	21	43	48	-5	43
16.	**Aston Villa**	38	10	12	16	42	55	-13	42
17.	Portsmouth	38	10	8	20	37	62	-25	38
18.	Birmingham City	38	8	10	20	28	50	-22	34
19.	West Bromwich Albion	38	7	9	22	31	58	-27	30
20.	Sunderland	38	3	6	29	26	69	-43	15

2005/06

Total
Played	Won	Drawn	Lost	points
38	10 (26 %)	12 (32 %)	16 (42 %)	42

Home
Played	Won	Drawn	Lost	points
19	6 (32 %)	6 (32 %)	7 (37 %)	24

Away
Played	Won	Drawn	Lost	points
19	4 (21 %)	6 (32 %)	9 (47 %)	18

Biggest home win
Dec 26th 2005 Aston Villa   4-0   Everton

Biggest home loss
Oct 22nd 2005 Aston Villa   0-2   Wigan Athletic
Nov 5th 2005   Aston Villa   0-2   Liverpool
Dec 17th 2005 Aston Villa   0-2   Manchester Utd

Biggest away win
Feb 4th 2006   Middlesbrough   0-4   Aston Villa

Biggest away loss
Apr 1st 2006   Arsenal   5-0   Aston Villa

Highest aggregate score home
Oct 2nd 2005   Aston Villa   2-3   Middlesbrough

Highest aggregate score away
Dec 28th 2005 Fulham   3-3   Aston Villa

ASTON VILLA 2006/07 RESULTS AND FIXTURES

English Premier	19-08-2006	Arsenal	1-1	**Aston Villa**
English Premier	23-08-2006	**Aston Villa**	2-1	Reading
English Premier	27-08-2006	**Aston Villa**	2-0	Newcastle
English Premier	10-09-2006	West Ham	1-1	**Aston Villa**
English Premier	16-09-2006	Watford	0-0	**Aston Villa**
English Premier	23-09-2006	**Aston Villa**	2-0	Charlton
English Premier	30-09-2006	Chelsea	1-1	**Aston Villa**
English Premier	14-10-2006	**Aston Villa**	1-1	Tottenham
English Premier	21-10-2006	**Aston Villa**	1-1	Fulham
English Premier	28-10-2006	Liverpool	3-1	**Aston Villa**
English Premier	05-11-2006	**Aston Villa**	2-0	Blackburn
English Premier	11-11-2006	Everton	0-1	**Aston Villa**
English Premier	19-11-2006	Wigan	0-0	**Aston Villa**
English Premier	25-11-2006	**Aston Villa**	1-1	Middlesbro
English Premier	29-11-2006	**Aston Villa**	1-3	Man City
English Premier	02-12-2006	Portsmouth	2-2	**Aston Villa**
English Premier	11-12-2006	Sheff Utd	2-2	**Aston Villa**
English Premier	16-12-2006	**Aston Villa**	0-1	Bolton
English Premier	23-12-2006	**Aston Villa**	0-3	Man Utd
English Premier	26-12-2006	Tottenham	2-1	**Aston Villa**
English Premier	30-12-2006	Charlton	2-1	**Aston Villa**
English Premier	02-01-2007	**Aston Villa**	0-0	Chelsea
English Premier	13-01-2007	Man Utd	3-1	**Aston Villa**
English Premier	20-01-2007	**Aston Villa**	2-0	Watford
English Premier	31-01-2007	Newcastle	3-1	**Aston Villa**
English Premier	03-02-2007	**Aston Villa**	1-0	West Ham
English Premier	10-02-2007	Reading	2-0	**Aston Villa**
English Premier	03-03-2007	Fulham	1-1	**Aston Villa**
English Premier	14-03-2007	**Aston Villa**	0-1	Arsenal
English Premier	18-03-2007	**Aston Villa**	0-0	Liverpool
English Premier	02-04-2007	**Aston Villa**	1-1	Everton
English Premier	07-04-2007	Blackburn	1-2	**Aston Villa**
English Premier	09-04-2007	**Aston Villa**	1-1	Wigan
English Premier	14-04-2007	Middlesbro	1-3	**Aston Villa**
English Premier	22-04-2007	**Aston Villa**	0-0	Portsmouth
English Premier	28-04-2007	Man City	0-2	**Aston Villa**
English Premier	05-05-2007	**Aston Villa**	3-0	Sheff Utd
English Premier	13-05-2007	Bolton	2-2	**Aston Villa**

THE VILLA PREMIER YEARS - 1992-2010

Pos	Club	P	W	D	L	F	A	GD	Pts
1.	Manchester United	38	27	6	5	80	22	58	87
2.	Chelsea	38	25	10	3	65	26	39	85
3.	Arsenal	38	24	11	3	74	31	43	83
4.	Liverpool	38	21	13	4	67	28	39	76
5.	Everton	38	19	8	11	55	33	22	65
6.	**Aston Villa**	**38**	**16**	**12**	**10**	**71**	**51**	**20**	**60**
7.	Blackburn Rovers	38	15	13	10	50	48	2	58
8.	Portsmouth	38	16	9	13	48	40	8	57
9.	Manchester City	38	15	10	13	45	53	-8	55
10.	West Ham United	38	13	10	15	42	50	-8	49
11.	Tottenham Hotspur	38	11	13	14	66	61	5	46
12.	Newcastle United	38	11	10	17	45	65	-20	43
13.	Middlesbrough	38	10	12	16	43	53	-10	42
14.	Wigan Athletic	38	10	10	18	34	51	-17	40
15.	Sunderland	38	11	6	21	36	59	-23	39
16.	Bolton Wanderers	38	9	10	19	36	54	-18	37
17.	Fulham	38	8	12	18	38	60	-22	36
18.	Reading	38	10	6	22	41	66	-25	36
19.	Birmingham City	38	8	11	19	46	62	-16	35
20.	Derby County	38	1	8	29	20	89	-69	11

Total
Played	**Won**	**Drawn**	**Lost**	**points**
38	11 (29 %)	17 (45 %)	10 (26 %)	50

Home
Played	**Won**	**Drawn**	**Lost**	**points**
19	7 (37 %)	8 (42 %)	4 (21 %)	29

Away
Played	**Won**	**Drawn**	**Lost**	**points**
19	4 (21 %)	9 (47 %)	6 (32 %)	21

Biggest home win
May 5th 2007   Aston Villa   3-0   Sheffield United

Biggest home loss
Dec 23rd 2006 Aston Villa   0-3   Manchester Utd

Biggest away win
Apr 14th 2007 Middlesbrough   1-3   Aston Villa
Apr 28th 2007 Manchester City   0-2   Aston Villa

Biggest away loss
Oct 28th 2006 Liverpool   3-1   Aston Villa
Jan 13th 2007 Manchester Utd   3-1   Aston Villa
Jan 31st 2007 Newcastle Utd   3-1   Aston Villa
Feb 10th 2007 Reading   2-0   Aston Villa

Highest aggregate score home
Nov 29th 2006 Aston Villa   1-3   Manchester City

Highest aggregate score away
Oct 28th 2006 Liverpool   3-1   Aston Villa
Dec 2nd 2006   Portsmouth   2-2   Aston Villa
Dec 11th 2006 Sheffield United   2-2   Aston Villa
Jan 13th 2007 Manchester Utd   3-1   Aston Villa
Jan 31st 2007 Newcastle Utd   3-1   Aston Villa
Apr 14th 2007 Middlesbrough   1-3   Aston Villa
May 13th 2007 Bolton Wanderers   2-2   Aston Villa

ASTON VILLA 2007/08 RESULTS AND FIXTURES

English Premier	11-08-2007	**Aston Villa**	1-2	Liverpool
English Premier	18-08-2007	Newcastle	0-0	**Aston Villa**
English Premier	25-08-2007	**Aston Villa**	2-1	Fulham
English Premier	02-09-2007	**Aston Villa**	2-0	Chelsea
English Premier	16-09-2007	Man City	1-0	**Aston Villa**
English Premier	23-09-2007	**Aston Villa**	2-0	Everton
English Premier	01-10-2007	Tottenham	4-4	**Aston Villa**
English Premier	06-10-2007	**Aston Villa**	1-0	West Ham
English Premier	20-10-2007	**Aston Villa**	1-4	Man Utd
English Premier	28-10-2007	Bolton	1-1	**Aston Villa**
English Premier	03-11-2007	**Aston Villa**	2-0	Derby
English Premier	11-11-2007	Birmingham	1-2	**Aston Villa**
English Premier	24-11-2007	Middlesbro	0-3	**Aston Villa**
English Premier	28-11-2007	Blackburn	0-4	**Aston Villa**
English Premier	01-12-2007	**Aston Villa**	1-2	Arsenal
English Premier	08-12-2007	**Aston Villa**	1-3	Portsmouth
English Premier	15-12-2007	Sunderland	1-1	**Aston Villa**
English Premier	22-12-2007	**Aston Villa**	1-1	Man City
English Premier	26-12-2007	Chelsea	4-4	**Aston Villa**
English Premier	29-12-2007	Wigan	1-2	**Aston Villa**
English Premier	01-01-2008	**Aston Villa**	2-1	Tottenham
English Premier	12-01-2008	**Aston Villa**	3-1	Reading
English Premier	21-01-2008	Liverpool	2-2	**Aston Villa**
English Premier	26-01-2008	**Aston Villa**	1-1	Blackburn
English Premier	03-02-2008	Fulham	2-1	**Aston Villa**
English Premier	09-02-2008	**Aston Villa**	4-1	Newcastle
English Premier	24-02-2008	Reading	1-2	**Aston Villa**
English Premier	01-03-2008	Arsenal	1-1	**Aston Villa**
English Premier	12-03-2008	**Aston Villa**	1-1	Middlesbro
English Premier	15-03-2008	Portsmouth	2-0	**Aston Villa**
English Premier	22-03-2008	**Aston Villa**	0-1	Sunderland
English Premier	29-03-2008	Man Utd	4-0	**Aston Villa**
English Premier	05-04-2008	**Aston Villa**	4-0	Bolton
English Premier	12-04-2008	Derby	0-6	**Aston Villa**
English Premier	20-04-2008	**Aston Villa**	5-1	Birmingham
English Premier	27-04-2008	Everton	2-2	**Aston Villa**
English Premier	03-05-2008	**Aston Villa**	0-2	Wigan
English Premier	11-05-2008	West Ham	2-2	**Aston Villa**

THE VILLA PREMIER YEARS - 1992-2010

Pos	Club	P	W	D	L	F	A	GD	Pts
1.	Manchester United	38	28	5	5	83	27	56	89
2.	Chelsea	38	24	11	3	64	24	40	83
3.	Liverpool	38	20	8	10	57	27	30	68
4.	Arsenal	38	19	11	8	63	35	28	68
5.	Tottenham Hotspur	38	17	9	12	57	54	3	60
6.	Everton	38	15	13	10	52	36	16	58
7.	Bolton Wanderers	38	16	8	14	47	52	-5	56
8.	Reading	38	16	7	15	52	47	5	55
9.	Portsmouth	38	14	12	12	45	42	3	54
10.	Blackburn Rovers	38	15	7	16	52	54	-2	52
11.	Aston Villa	38	11	17	10	43	41	2	50
12.	Middlesbrough	38	12	10	16	44	49	-5	46
13.	Newcastle United	38	11	10	17	38	47	-9	43
14.	Manchester City	38	11	9	18	29	44	-15	42
15.	West Ham United	38	12	5	21	35	59	-24	41
16.	Fulham	38	8	15	15	38	60	-22	39
17.	Wigan Athletic	38	10	8	20	37	59	-22	38
18.	Sheffield United	38	10	8	20	32	55	-23	38
19.	Charlton Athletic	38	8	10	20	34	60	-26	34
20.	Watford	38	5	13	20	29	59	-30	28

Total

Played	Won	Drawn	Lost	points
38	16 (42 %)	12 (32 %)	10 (26 %)	60

Home

Played	Won	Drawn	Lost	points
19	10 (53 %)	3 (16 %)	6 (32 %)	33

Away

Played	Won	Drawn	Lost	points
19	6 (32 %)	9 (47 %)	4 (21 %)	27

THE VILLA PREMIER YEARS - 1992-2010

Biggest home win
Apr 5th 2008   Aston Villa   4-0   Bolton Wanderers
Apr 20th 2008 Aston Villa   5-1   Birmingham City

Biggest home loss
Oct 20th 2007 Aston Villa   1-4   Manchester Utd

Biggest away win
Apr 12th 2008 Derby County   0-6   Aston Villa

Biggest away loss
Mar 29th 2008 Manchester Utd   4-0   Aston Villa

Highest aggregate score home
Apr 20th 2008 Aston Villa   5-1   Birmingham City

Highest aggregate score away
Oct 1st 2007   Tottenham H.   4-4   Aston Villa
Dec 26th 2007 Chelsea   4-4   Aston Villa

ASTON VILLA 2008/09 RESULTS AND FIXTURES

DATE	OPPONENT	RESULT	SCORE
17.08.2008	Manchester City	W	4-2
23.08.2008	Stoke City	L	2-3
31.08.2008	Liverpool	D	0-0
15.09.2008	Tottenham Hotspur	W	2-1
21.09.2008	West Bromwich Albion	W	2-1
27.09.2008	Sunderland	W	2-1
05.10.2008	Chelsea	L	0-2
18.10.2008	Portsmouth	D	0-0
26.10.2008	Wigan Athletic	W	4-0
29.10.2008	Blackburn Rovers	W	3-2
03.11.2008	Newcastle United	L	0-2
09.11.2008	Middlesbrough	L	1-2
15.11.2008	Arsenal	W	2-0
22.11.2008	Manchester United	D	0-0
29.11.2008	Fulham	D	0-0
07.12.2008	Everton	W	3-2
13.12.2008	Bolton Wanderers	W	4-2
20.12.2008	West Ham United	W	1-0
26.12.2008	Arsenal	D	2-2
30.12.2008	Hull City	W	1-0
10.01.2009	West Bromwich Albion	W	2-1
17.01.2009	Sunderland	W	2-1
27.01.2009	Portsmouth	W	1-0
31.01.2009	Wigan Athletic	D	0-0
07.02.2009	Blackburn Rovers	W	2-0
21.02.2009	Chelsea	L	0-1
01.03.2009	Stoke City	D	2-2
04.03.2009	Manchester City	L	0-2
15.03.2009	Tottenham Hotspur	L	1-2
22.03.2009	Liverpool	L	0-5
05.04.2009	Manchester United	L	2-3
12.04.2009	Everton	D	3-3
18.04.2009	West Ham United	D	1-1
25.04.2009	Bolton Wanderers	D	1-1
04.05.2009	Hull City	W	1-0
09.05.2009	Fulham	L	1-3
16.05.2009	Middlesbrough	D	1-1
24.05.2009	Newcastle United	W	1-0

THE VILLA PREMIER YEARS - 1992-2010

Pos	Club	P	W	D	L	F	A	GD	Pts
1.	Manchester United	38	28	6	4	68	24	44	90
2.	Liverpool	38	25	11	2	77	27	50	86
3.	Chelsea	38	25	8	5	68	24	44	83
4.	Arsenal	38	20	12	6	68	37	31	72
5.	Everton	38	17	12	9	55	37	18	63
6.	Aston Villa	38	17	11	10	54	48	6	62
7.	Fulham	38	14	11	13	39	34	5	53
8.	Tottenham Hotspur	38	14	9	15	45	45	0	51
9.	West Ham United	38	14	9	15	42	45	-3	51
10.	Manchester City	38	15	5	18	58	50	8	50
11.	Wigan Athletic	38	12	9	17	34	45	-11	45
12.	Stoke City	38	12	9	17	38	55	-17	45
13.	Bolton Wanderers	38	11	8	19	41	53	-12	41
14.	Portsmouth	38	10	11	17	38	57	-19	41
15.	Blackburn Rovers	38	10	11	17	40	60	-20	41
16.	Sunderland	38	9	9	20	34	54	-20	36
17.	Hull City	38	8	11	19	39	64	-25	35
18.	Newcastle United	38	7	13	18	40	59	-19	34
19.	Middlesbrough	38	7	11	20	28	57	-29	32
20.	West Bromwich Albion	38	8	8	22	36	67	-31	32

2008/09

Total
Played	Won	Drawn	Lost	Points
38	17 (45 %)	11 (29 %)	10 (26 %)	62

Home
Played	Won	Drawn	Lost	Points
19	7 (37 %)	9 (47 %)	3 (16 %)	30

Away
Played	Won	Drawn	Lost	Points
19	10 (53 %)	2 (11 %)	7 (37 %)	32

Biggest home win

Aug 17th 2008	Aston Villa	4-2	Manchester City
Dec 13th 2008	Aston Villa	4-2	Bolton Wanderers

Biggest home loss

Nov 9th 2008	Aston Villa	1-2	Middlesbrough
Feb 21st 2009	Aston Villa	0-1	Chelsea
Mar 15th 2009	Aston Villa	1-2	Tottenham H.

Biggest away win

Oct 26th 2008	Wigan A.	0-4	Aston Villa

Biggest away loss

Mar 22nd 2009	Liverpool	5-0	Aston Villa

Highest aggregate score home

Aug 17th 2008	Aston Villa	4-2	Manchester City
Dec 13th 2008	Aston Villa	4-2	Bolton Wanderers
Apr 12th 2009	Aston Villa	3-3	Everton

Highest aggregate score away

Aug 23rd 2008	Stoke City	3-2	Aston Villa
Dec 7th 2008	Everton	2-3	Aston Villa
Mar 22nd 2009	Liverpool	5-0	Aston Villa
Apr 5th 2009	Manchester Utd	3-2	Aston Villa

THE VILLA PREMIER YEARS - 1992-2010

A Selection of Memorable Premier League Games

15-08-1992 **Ipswich** **1-1** **Aston Villa**
Johnson 31   *Atkinson 84*

Our First Ever Game In The Premier League.

19-09-1992 **Aston Villa** **4-2** **Liverpool**
Saunders 44, 66   *Walters 43*
Atkinson 54   *Rosenthal 84*
Parker 78

Big game for deano v his old club.

17-01-1993 **Aston Villa** **5-1** **Middlesbro**
Parker 26   *Hignett 82*
Mcgrath 32
Yorke 44
Saunders 58
Teale 68

This was a great performance with great well worked goals.

14-08-1993 **Aston Villa** **4-1** **QPR**
Atkinson 38, 89   *Ferdinand 45*
Saunders 62
Staunton 90

This was one of my favourite early games, I remember sitting in the Doug Ellis stand watching this one with my father.

12-02-1994 **Aston Villa** **5-0** **Swindon**
Saunders 31, 66, 84
Froggatt 55
Richardson 73

I remember watching this one with my cousin Joe and Our great nan, we were sat in the doug ellis upper, I remember one of deano's goals was about 30 yards out and flew into the top corner.

07-05-1994 **Aston Villa** **2-1** **Liverpool**
Yorke 65, 81   *Fowler 17*

I think everyone remembers this one, it was the last game where the famous Holte End was Standing, it was a great game, non – stop bouncing in the Holte all game.

THE VILLA PREMIER YEARS - 1992-2010

19-11-1994	**Tottenham**	**3-4**	**Aston Villa**
	Bosnich og		Atkinson
	Klinsmann		Fenton x2
	Sheringham		Saunders

What a game, I remember listening to this on the radio at my stepdad's moms, I just remember running around telling all the family eachtime we scored, running in yelling loud.

11-02-1995	**Aston Villa**	**7-1**	**Wimbledon**
	Johnson x3		Barton
	Reeves og		
	Saunders x2		
	Yorke		

This was incredible, I was distraught though as I had the chance by my father to choose to go against wimbledon or Leicester, guess which 1 I picked ?

22-02-1995	**Aston Villa**	**4-4**	**Leicester**
	Johnson		Lowe x 2
	Saunders		Roberts
	Staunton		Robins
	Yorke		

Yes, you guessed it I chose the Leicester game, we was 4-1 up, I was absolutely gutted I actually had tears as we clapped the players off, there was the odd boo aswell of course, throwing away a lead like that wasn't a good thing.

19-08-1995	**Aston Villa**	**3-1**	**Man Utd**
	Taylor 14		Beckham 82
	Draper 27		
	Yorke 36		

This was Draper's debut and Savo's, it was a new look Villa Team and beating Man United was awesome, I was gutted though as I missed this one due to a caravan holiday with the parents, great eh.

16-12-1995	**Aston Villa**	**4-1**	**Coventry**
	Johnson 12		Dublin 54
	Milosevic 48, 64, 80		

Wow Savo scored a hat-trick, he didn't score many but this was definitely his afternoon, I was in the Upper Holte for this one where I stayed now forever, Dion Dublin scored for Coventry, have you heard of him ?

THE VILLA PREMIER YEARS - 1992-2010

21-01-1996 **Aston Villa** **2-1** **Tottenham**
McGrath 23 Fox 26
Yorke 79

Dwight scored a wonder goal, it started outside the box and he took everyone on, it ended in a great goal from a tight angle, This was also televised.

30-09-1996 **Newcastle** **4-3** **Aston Villa**
Ferdinand 5, 22 Yorke 4, 59, 69
Shearer 38
Howey 67

This was a great performance, Yorke getting a hat-trick away from home and still not winning, Newcastle were a great side back then, I watched this at my Grandad's- RIP, It was on Sky Monday Night Football.

22-12-1996 **Aston Villa** **5-0** **Wimbledon**
Yorke 38, 86
Milosevic 42, 75
Taylor 61

This was a great game with great goals in each half, we totally dominated, Wimbledon hardly touched the ball.

26-12-1997 **Aston Villa** **4-1** **Tottenham**
Draper 38, 68 Calderwood 59
Collymore 81, 89

This was televised, Merry Christmas, Villa park was rocking, great atmosphere and to see Big Stan scoring twice was great, and Calderwood was a future Villa player.

10-05-1998 **Aston Villa** **1-0** **Arsenal**
Yorke 37

I'm sure everyone remembers this one, Dwight's cheeky chipped penalty down the middle, a great way to end the season

07-11-1998 **Aston Villa** **3-2** **Tottenham**
Dublin 31, 35 Anderton 65
Collymore 48 Vega 76

Dion's debut, every villa fan was excited when we signed him, he was the sort of big player we needed and we were excited to see his partnership with Collymore.

14-11-1998	**Southampton**	**1-4**	**Aston Villa**	
	Le Tissier 53		Dublin 3, 56, 85	
			Merson 77	

Dion carried on his amazing start in a villa shirt, a awesome hat-trick away from home, I was at my dad's listening to this one on the radio.

13-12-1998	**Aston Villa**	**3-2**	**Arsenal**	
	Joachim 62		Bergkamp 14, 45	
	Dublin 65, 83			

What a memorable game, we were 2-0 down at half-time, and super Dion won it for us again.

17-04-1999	**Liverpool**	**0-1**	**Aston Villa**	
			Taylor 33	

A rare win at Anfield, "There's only one Ian Taylor".

05-02-2000	**Aston Villa**	**4-0**	**Watford**	
	Stone 47			
	Merson 57, 59			
	Walker 81			

It was 0-0 at half-time, we came out 2nd half and we were a different team, merson's one goal was a great lob outside the box, and a young Richard Walker scored also.

14-02-2000	**Middlesbro**	**0-4**	**Aston Villa**	
			Carbone 11, 65	
			Joachim 70, 75	

Carbone ohhhh, Carbone ohhhh. What a great player he was, one of his more memorable goals was against Leeds in the fa cup at home, a 40 yarder, but this game he was awesome.

15-04-2000	**Tottenham**	**2-4**	**Aston Villa**	
	Iversen 16		Dublin 62, 69	
	Armstrong 47		Carbone 70	
			Wright 74	

Alan Wright scored a screamer outside the box 40 yards, carbone's was a over headkick if I remember right, a great performance, we were 2-0 down again at half time but a remarkable come back.

27-08-2000	**Aston Villa**	**1-1**	**Chelsea**	
	Nilis 10		Desailly 30	

THE VILLA PREMIER YEARS - 1992-2010

The wonderful Left footed goal and turn from Luc Nilis, he looked great for us at the start, we all know what happened next.

09-09-2000	**Ipswich**	**1-2**	**Aston Villa**
	Stewart 90		Hendrie 28
			Dublin 54

What a sad day this was, I can still picture the horror tackle which involved goalkeeper Richard Wright, Luc Nilis only just joined us and this was his last game in his career as he broke his leg.

17-04-2001	**Charlton**	**3-3**	**Aston Villa**
	Boateng 16 og		Ginola 59
	Jensen 45		Vassell 75
	Kinsella 89		Hendrie 90

We were 2-0 down at half-time AGAIN, then a bit of magic from Ginola and a good goal from darius made it 2-2, but a future villa player mark kinsella scored with 1 minute to go and it felt cruel as we pulled it back and it's a horrible feeling to lose with 1 minute to go, but then hendrie popped up with another equaliser.

05-05-2001	**Aston Villa**	**3-2**	**Coventry**
	Vassell 61		Hadji 18, 26
	Angel 81		
	Merson 86		

What a game, we were 2 goals down at half time again, we pulled it back to 2-2, then out of nowhere Magic Merse scored a 30 Yard screamer outside the box straight into the top corner, the holte end was electric, I was so proud, I remember having a few tears at the end, I'm too emotional ha. We sent Coventry down too and they haven't been back since.

08-09-2001	**Liverpool**	**1-3**	**Aston Villa**
	Gerrard 46		Dublin 31
			Hendrie 55
			Vassell 86

No one expected us to win this, it was a great result as it's so hard to go to Anfield and win.

27-10-2001	**Aston Villa**	**3-2**	**Bolton**
	Angel 13, 47		Ricketts 2, 75
	Vassell 43		

This game took us top of the Premier League, we went on a great run.

11-05-2002	Chelsea	1-3	Aston Villa
	Gudjohnsen 70		Crouch 21
			Vassell 63
			Dublin 88

This was a great result away from home, Chelsea was a hard place to go too even back then.

14-12-2002	Aston Villa	2-1	West Brom
	Vassell 16		Koumas 29
	Hitzlsperger 90		

It was great having a real local derby again, and it was a awesome atmosphere, and I can still picture Tommy's wonder goal now, it screamed into the Keepers right top corner, Cracking goal to win a derby in the last minute.

28-01-2003	Middlesbro	2-5	Aston Villa
	Maccarone 33		Vassell 24, 81
	Greening 35		Gudjohnsen 31
			Barry 48
			Dublin 90

Graham Taylor's era, Joey scored a screamer and it was a great emphatic result away from home.

19-04-2003	Aston Villa	2-1	Chelsea
	Allback 11, 78		Terry 89

A Rare double from Marcus Allback, a great game with a great result to match.

14-12-2003	Aston Villa	3-2	Wolves
	Angel 21, 24		Rae 36
	Barry 48		Kennedy 80

It was great to see the wolves back in the bigtime, I love our games v the wolves, this was a hard game, but was delighted we got the result.

31-01-2004	Leicester	0-5	Aston Villa
			Vassell 50, 60
			Crouch 57, 68
			Dublin 64

I was there, Jim Walker our old physio was sat behind me, it was a wonderful second half, the stewards told me to calm down ha, I was close to the supporter who got on the pitch and started on Ian Walker, This was solano's debut also.

14-03-2004   **Wolves   0-4   Aston Villa**
                                       Hitzlesperger 7
                                       Mellberg 18
                                       Angel 24, 59

This was a awesome result, Angels 2nd goal was quality, I remember walking out the ground and had to walk in between 2 wolves pubs rammed, his woman had a cheeseburger full of sauce thrown in her face nice !!

13-08-2005   **Aston Villa   2-2   Bolton**
                     Phillips 4   Davies 6
                     Davis 9   Campo 8

The game was over after 9 minutes, it was a bizarre start to the season, just a shame we didn't win after.

16-10-2005   **Birmingham   0-1   Aston Villa**
                                            Phillips 19

Super super kev, super super kev, super super kev, super Kevin Phillips, our first win against them in the premiership.

26-12-2005   **Aston Villa   4-0   Everton**
                     Baros 35, 84
                     Delaney 48
                     Angel 82

A great festive game, Baros played great, it was a rare great performance by him.

28-12-2005   **Fulham   3-3   Aston Villa**
                     McBride 13, 61   Moore 29
                     Helguson 32   Ridgewell 60, 76

This was a great game, villa just kept coming back, Ridgewell scored a few goals for us but a lot of mistakes too giving away penalties and scoring own goals.

02-01-2006   **West Brom   1-2   Aston Villa**
                     Watson 76   Davis 47
                                             Baros 80

Another great derby win for us, I was gutted at the time I couldn't go as I was working in a bookies and they wouldn't give me the time off great eh !

THE VILLA PREMIER YEARS - 1992-2010

04-02-2006 Middlesbro 0-4 **Aston Villa**
                                  Moore 18, 62, 64
                                  Phillips 24

This was a awesome away day, this was the game where a Boro supporter came on the pitch and threw his season ticket, Luke Moore had a great day.

16-04-2006 **Aston Villa** 3-1 Birmingham
                Baros 10, 78   Sutton 25
                Cahill 56

What a goal by Gary Cahill, we should never of sold him, That goal will always be remembered until Eternity, what a amazing day.

19-08-2006 Arsenal   1-1 **Aston Villa**
                Gilberto 84   Mellberg 53

Martin O'Neill's first game in charge, a fantastic result which was also Arsenal's first game at the Emirates stadium.

23-08-2006 **Aston Villa** 2-1 Reading
                Angel 34   Doyle 4
                Barry 61

Martin's first home game for us, we didn't start well but it was great to win in the end and a great start to Martin's Villa Career.

30-09-2006 Chelsea   1-1 **Aston Villa**
                Drogba 3   Agbonlahor 45

A great result, Chelsea were flying at the time so it was great to go to one of the big boys and perform like we did and get a great result.

05-05-2007 **Aston Villa** 3-0 Sheff Utd
                Agbonlahor 25
                A.Young 42
                Berger 59

This was a awesome atmosphere, it was our last home game of the season and Berger scored a real class goal, it was a wonderful afternoon ending Martin's first season in charge.

02-09-2007 **Aston Villa** 2-0 Chelsea
                Knight 47
                Agbonlahor 88

A awesome result, Knight's debut too, what a great start for the Villa fan.

THE VILLA PREMIER YEARS - 1992-2010

01-10-2007   **Tottenham**   **4-4**   **Aston Villa**
Berbatov 20   Laursen 22, 33
Chimbonda 69   Agbonlahor 40
Keane 82   Gardner 59
Kaboul 90

I was gutted, we was 4-1 up, I remember kicking a vase over in my living room, it was on the cards towards the end, you could see it coming.

11-11-2007   **Birmingham**   **1-2**   **Aston Villa**
Forssell 62   Ridgewell 11 og
     Agbonlahor 87

What a feeling this was, Super Gabby in the last minute, I remember going the Aston Social after till Midnight celebrating.

28-11-2007   **Blackburn**   **0-4**   **Aston Villa**
     Carew 29
     Barry 53
     Ash Young 81
     Harewood 89

This was a great result away from home, we were in a great run of form, Young's goal was awesome.

26-12-2007   **Chelsea**   **4-4**   **Aston Villa**
Shevchenko 45, 50   Maloney 14, 44
Alex 66   Laursen 72
Ballack 88   Barry 90

What a game, it was boxing day I was buzzing, I watched it with mates in The Royal in Sutton Coldfield it was packed, it was up and down all game, when Barry scored in the last Minute , it was one of the best feelings ever.

21-01-2008   **Liverpool**   **2-2**   **Aston Villa**
Benayoun 19   Harewood 69
Crouch 88   Aurelio 72 og

We was so close to a big upset, until crouchy scored with 2 minutes to go, that was a real gutting feeling, Marlon came on and scored a wonderful overhead kick, he was bang in form at the time.

09-02-2008   **Aston Villa**   **4-1**   **Newcastle**
Bouma 48   Owen 4
Carew 51, 72, 90

John Carew, Carew, He's bigger than me and you. A great day for big john.

THE VILLA PREMIER YEARS - 1992-2010

01-03-2008   **Arsenal**   **1-1**   **Aston Villa**
                 Bendtner 90   Senderos 27 og

Me and a few of the lads stayed overnight in London for this one, we was absolutely gutted when Bendtner scored in the last minute, I actually had a few tears I felt like we lost a cup final, proper gutted but it was still a great point at the end of the day.

12-04-2008   **Derby**   **0-6**   **Aston Villa**
                                       Ash Young 25
                                       Carew 26
                                       Petrov 36
                                       Barry 58
                                       Agbonlahor 76
                                       Harewood 85

What a game, 6 goals away from home, Petrov's goal was stunning over 30 yards out.

20-04-2008   **Aston Villa**   **5-1**   **Birmingham**
                 Ash Young 28, 63   Forssell 67
                 Carew 42, 53
                 Agbonlahor 78

This was a incredible game, I have'nt seen the goals since though as it reminds me of when my mate died after the game. RIP CHRIS PRIEST xxx

27-04-2008   **Everton**   **2-2**   **Aston Villa**
                 Neville 56   Agbonlahor 80
                 Yobo 84   Carew 86

This was a emotional game for a lot of people a lot of us went to the game, with a big flag dedicated to Chris Priest, who died the week before.

17-08-2008   **Aston Villa**   **4-2**   **Manchester City**
                 Carew 47   Elano 64
                 Agbonlahor 69, 74, 76   Corluka 89

Super Gabby with a rare Hat-trick, great atmosphere, and a great first game in charge of city for Mark Hughes.

21-09-2008   **West Brom**   **1-2**   **Aston Villa**
                 Morrison 34   Carew 27
                                           Agbonlahor 29

What a great 2 minutes for Villa, it was mad with 3 goals in 7 minutes then none for the rest of the game.

THE VILLA PREMIER YEARS - 1992-2010

26-10-2008   **Wigan Athletic**   **0-4**   **Aston Villa**
Barry 22   Agbonlahor 57
                              Carew 62
                              Sidwell 90

We had a coach load for this one, it was a great day out, sidwell's goal was a cracker after he came on as a sub, it was great to see him score after he was injured at first when we signed him.

15-11-2008   **Arsenal**   **0-2**   **Aston Villa**
                                       Clichy (og) 70
                                       Agbonlahor 80

Cracking result, Gabby played awesome, one of our best results of latter years.

07-12-2008   **Everton**   **2-3**   **Aston Villa**
Lescott 30, 90   Sidwell 1
                                     Ash Young 54, 90

What a game, I was so gutted when Lescott scored in the last minute I was going mad. You could see it happen though, and Villa sometimes throw it away in the last minute, but then Young ran onto a flick on by gabby, he went in and out of the defender then scored in the last second, everyone went ballistic, that will never be forgotten.

26-12-2008   **Aston Villa**   **2-2**   **Arsenal**
Barry 65   Denilson 40
Knight 90   Diaby 49

This was a very hard game, Arsenal were bang in form and we were flying at the top also, Zat Knight scored in the last minute and the ground was rocking.

10-01-2009   **Aston Villa**   **2-1**   **West Brom**
Davies 19   Morrison 49
Carson 41 og

Another great derby with Curtis scoring v his old club, and Carson coming back to score a own goal.

THE VILLA PREMIER YEARS - 1992-2010

12-04-2009 **Aston Villa** **3-3** **Everton**
Carew 33   Fellaini 19
Milner 55   Cahill 23
Barry 66   Pienaar 53

We went 3-1 down, so it was great character to pull it back to 3-3, we needed to win this one though with us both fighting for the European places.

24-05-2009 **Aston Villa** **1-0** **Newcastle United**
Duff 38 og

This was a average kind of game, but it was great that we sent a big team down as Newcastle was relegated.

24-08-2009 **Liverpool** **1-3** **Aston Villa**
Torres 72   Lucas 34 og
                                  Davies 45
                                  Ash Young 75

This was great, everyone expected Liverpool to beat us, especially as we lost to Wigan at home the week before. Villa played great.

13-09-2009 **Birmingham** **0-1** **Aston Villa**
                                  Agbonlahor 85

What a feeling, Gabby winning it for us again in the last few minutes.

05-10-2009 **Aston Villa** **1-1** **Manchester City**
Dunne 15   Bellamy 67

Richard Dunne scoring v His old team which was great, Man City full of expensive signings and we should of won this, but at the time it was a good result televised too.

17-10-2009 **Aston Villa** **2-1** **Chelsea**
Dunne 32   Drogba 15
Collins 52

Another Great result v the big 4, I was in china for this one so I was gutted I was missing such a big game, and both our centre backs scoring. Awesome.

07-11-2009　　**Aston Villa**　　**5-1**　　**Bolton**
　　　　　　　　　Ash Young 5　　　　　*Elmander 44*
　　　　　　　　　Agbonlahor 43
　　　　　　　　　Carew 53
　　　　　　　　　Milner 72
　　　　　　　　　Cuellar 75

This was a great performance, poor Cahill and Knight coming back, they had a horrid afternoon.

12-12-2009　　**Manchester United**　　**0-1**　　**Aston Villa**
　　　　　　　　　　　　　　　　　　　　　　　　　　Agbonlahor 21

Never been so chuffed in all my life I was sweating in the last 20 minutes, because united always come back against us, like the Macheda goal the season before against us when they won in the last minute. Absolutly wonderful performance, so so proud. Another big team scalp this season.

First Days of every season

15-08-1992	Ipswich	1-1	Aston Villa
14-08-1993	Aston Villa	4-1	QPR
20-08-1994	Everton	2-2	Aston Villa
19-08-1995	Aston Villa	3-1	Man Utd
17-08-1996	Sheff Wed	2-1	Aston Villa
09-08-1997	Leicester	1-0	Aston Villa
15-08-1998	Everton	0-0	Aston Villa
07-08-1999	Newcastle	0-1	Aston Villa
19-08-2000	Leicester	0-0	Aston Villa
18-08-2001	Tottenham	0-0	Aston Villa
18-08-2002	Aston Villa	0-1	Liverpool
16-08-2003	Portsmouth	2-1	Aston Villa
14-08-2004	Aston Villa	2-0	Southampton
13-08-2005	Aston Villa	2-2	Bolton
19-08-2006	Arsenal	1-1	Aston Villa
11-08-2007	Aston Villa	1-2	Liverpool
17-08-2008	Aston Villa	4-2	Man City

Villa's Results v Midlands Teams

Aston Villa	2-1	Nottm Forest	12-12-1992
Coventry	3-0	Aston Villa	26-12-1992
Nott'm Forest	0-1	Aston Villa	04-04-1993
Aston Villa	0-0	Coventry	10-04-1993
Aston Villa	0-0	Coventry	11-09-1993
Coventry	0-1	Aston Villa	06-03-1994
Coventry	0-1	Aston Villa	29-08-1994
Aston Villa	0-2	Nottm Forest	22-10-1994
Leicester	1-1	Aston Villa	03-12-1994
Nott'm Forest	1-2	Aston Villa	21-01-1995
Aston Villa	4-4	Leicester	22-02-1995
Aston Villa	0-0	Coventry	06-03-1995
Aston Villa	1-1	Nott'm Forest	23-09-1995
Coventry	0-3	Aston Villa	30-09-1995
Nottm Forest	1-1	Aston Villa	10-12-1995
Aston Villa	4-1	Coventry	16-12-1995
Aston Villa	2-0	Derby	24-08-1996
Aston Villa	2-0	Nottm Forest	02-11-1996
Aston Villa	1-3	Leicester	16-11-1996

THE VILLA PREMIER YEARS - 1992-2010

Coventry	1-2		Aston Villa	23-11-1996
Aston Villa	2-1		Coventry	19-02-1997
Nottm Forest	0-0		Aston Villa	22-02-1997
Leicester	1-0		Aston Villa	05-03-1997
Derby	2-1		Aston Villa	12-04-1997
Leicester	1-0		Aston Villa	09-08-1997
Aston Villa	2-1		Derby	20-09-1997
Aston Villa	3-0		Coventry	06-12-1997
Aston Villa	1-1		Leicester	10-01-1998
Derby	0-1		Aston Villa	07-02-1998
Coventry	1-2		Aston Villa	11-04-1998
Aston Villa	1-0		Derby	26-09-1998
Coventry	1-2		Aston Villa	03-10-1998
Aston Villa	1-1		Leicester	24-10-1998
Nott'm Forest	2-2		Aston Villa	28-11-1998
Aston Villa	1-4		Coventry	27-02-1999
Derby	2-1		Aston Villa	10-03-1999
Leicester	2-2		Aston Villa	06-04-1999
Aston Villa	2-0		Nottm Forest	24-04-1999
Leicester	3-1		Aston Villa	25-09-1999
Coventry	2-1		Aston Villa	22-11-1999
Derby	0-2		Aston Villa	26-12-1999
Aston Villa	1-0		Coventry	11-03-2000
Aston Villa	2-0		Derby	25-03-2000
Aston Villa	2-2		Leicester	22-04-2000
Leicester	0-0		Aston Villa	19-08-2000
Aston Villa	4-1		Derby	30-09-2000
Coventry	1-1		Aston Villa	25-11-2000
Derby	1-0		Aston Villa	24-02-2001
Aston Villa	2-1		Leicester	04-04-2001
Aston Villa	3-2		Coventry	05-05-2001
Aston Villa	0-2		Leicester	01-12-2001
Derby	3-1		Aston Villa	22-12-2001
Aston Villa	2-1		Derby	12-01-2002
Leicester	2-2		Aston Villa	20-04-2002
Birmingham	3-0		Aston Villa	16-09-2002
West Brom	0-0		Aston Villa	16-11-2002
Aston Villa	2-1		West Brom	14-12-2002
Aston Villa	0-2		Birmingham	03-03-2003
Aston Villa	3-1		Leicester	30-08-2003
Birmingham	0-0		Aston Villa	19-10-2003

THE VILLA PREMIER YEARS - 1992-2010

Aston Villa	3-2	Wolves	14-12-2003
Leicester	0-5	Aston Villa	31-01-2004
Aston Villa	2-2	Birmingham	22-02-2004
Wolves	0-4	Aston Villa	14-03-2004
West Brom	1-1	Aston Villa	22-08-2004
Aston Villa	1-2	Birmingham	12-12-2004
Birmingham	2-0	Aston Villa	20-03-2005
Aston Villa	1-1	West Brom	10-04-2005
Birmingham	0-1	Aston Villa	16-10-2005
West Brom	1-2	Aston Villa	02-01-2006
Aston Villa	0-0	West Brom	09-04-2006
Aston Villa	3-1	Birmingham	16-04-2006
Aston Villa	2-0	Derby	03-11-2007
Birmingham	1-2	Aston Villa	11-11-2007
Derby	0-6	Aston Villa	12-04-2008
Aston Villa	5-1	Birmingham	20-04-2008
Stoke City	3-2	Aston Villa	23-08-2008
West Brom	1-2	Aston Villa	21-09-2008
Aston Villa	2-1	West Brom	10-01-2009
Aston Villa	2-2	Stoke City	01-03-2009

VILLA'S PREMIER BEST XI

BOSNICH

MELLBERG LAURSEN MCGRATH STAUNTON

MILNER MERSON TAYLOR YOUNG

YORKE SAUNDERS

OTHER EMPIRE PUBLICATIONS

BACK FROM THE BRINK
by Justin Blundell
The Untold story of Manchester United in the Depression Years 1919-32

SPECIAL OFFER: £8
PAPERBACK

IN THE RICH HISTORY OF MANCHESTER UNITED THERE HAVE BEEN SEVERAL GREAT CRISES - BACK FROM THE BRINK TELLS THE STORY OF THE MOST SIGNIFICANT OF THEM ALL...

If Manchester United revelled in innocent childhood during the Edwardian era, winning two league titles and an FA Cup within 9 years of the club's establishment, it endured a painful adolescence as the inter-war years saw it absent from the honours lists. In this amusing, irreverent and fascinating account, Justin Blundell traces the events of the club's lost youth between the end of the Great War and the worldwide economic crisis that almost scuppered the club yet ushered in a new era under James Gibson.

Blundell's punchy account deserves to stand alongside the many volumes written about the post-war glory years - it tells the story of how United survived the Depression Years and came back from the brink.

Morrissey's Manchester
by Phill Gatenby
Second Edition

Lyrically unique, Morrissey saw 1980s Manchester differently. Where most recognised the derelict remains of a Victorian warehouse, he saw humour, where others saw post-industrial squalor, he felt the frisson of romance.
As a result the city became as much a part of The Smiths output as the guitars, drums and vocals. Unusually, these places still exist and provide the devotee with a place of pilgrimage. Now updated, Morrissey's Manchester has added new places to visit, more lyrical references and more background information on one of the world's most influential bands.

SPECIAL OFFER: £6
PAPERBACK

From Goal line to Touch-line
My Career with Manchester United
by Jack Crompton

Hardback
Special offer £12

Jack Crompton is one of the surviving members of Manchester United's swashbuckling 1948 FA Cup winning side and the first to pen his autobiography. Jack served the club as goalkeeper, trainer and caretaker manager for over 40 years playing a major part in the triumphs of the immediate post-war years and witnessed the rise of the Busby Babes first hand before leaving for a coaching role with Luton Town in 1956.
Now a sprightly octagenarian, Jack is in a unique position to discuss the considerable changes in the game during his lifetime and look back on a seven decade long association with Manchester United.

18 TIMES AND THAT'S A FACT!
BY JUSTIN BLUNDELL
400PP - PAPERBACK - £10.95

This was the season when Sir Alex Ferguson's long-held wish to 'knock Liverpool off their f**king perch' was made flesh. A season so successful that even European Cup Final defeat to Barcelona couldn't fully diminish the club's achievements. Justin Blundell tells the story of United's triumphs in a punchy, rabidly red-eyed review of every single match and goal.

Written with an eye for the humour and pomoposity surrounding the modern game, Justin Blundell brings the matches, goals and managerial spats back to life in an entertaining, minute-by-minute guide to the matches that really mattered. "18 times" is a book for everyone who lives and breathes United, not just on match day but every single day.

SPECIAL OFFER: £8 PAPERBACK

Memories... Of a Failed Footballer
AND A CRAP JOURNALIST
BY PAUL HINCE

PAUL HINCE BEGAN his football career with boyhood heroes Manchester City under the legendary Mercer-Allison partnership of the late 1960s before continuing his first class football career at Charlton, Bury and Crewe Alexandra. After retiring from the game he worked his way up to the heights of Manchester Evening News Manchester City correspondent and, later, that paper's first, and only, 'Chief Sports Writer'. Famed in later years for getting up the noses of both United and City fans in equal measure courtesy of his weekly columns, Paul retired from the Manchester Evening News in 2006.

SPECIAL OFFER £7

THE COMPLETE ERIC CANTONA
BY DARREN PHILLIPS
PUBLISHED: NOVEMBER 2009 - £10.95

ERIC CANTONA'S CAREER at Old Trafford lasted only 5 years but its lasting impact is still being felt today. During that comparatively small span, Cantona's dedication and self-confidence enabled a club to emerge from over a quarter of a century of failure and self-doubt. The Complete Eric Cantona details every game Eric played for Manchester United, Leeds United and the French national team as well as potted summaries of his career in France. Darren Phillips, author of The Complete George Best, has painstakingly researched his remarkable career in France, England and in the French national team.

SPECIAL OFFER: £8 PAPERBACK

Reminiscences of Manchester
And its surrounding areas from 1840
by Louis M Hayes - Originally published 1905

WRITTEN OVER THE course of his lifetime, Louis Hayes' memoirs of Manchester life 'Reminiscenes of Manchester' is an evocative look back at the city's formative years. As well as outlining the social changes in the city, Hayes profiles the key characters, many he knew personally, to make a mark in Manchester life.

An invaluable guide to those keen to know more about the formative years of the city and those who wonder what life was like for Mancunians over a century ago, Reminiscences of Manchester is a remarkable work re-printed here in full with additional footnotes and the illustrations published in the original edition.

special offer £9

PUBLISHED FEBRUARY 2010

OLD TRAFFORD
100 YEARS OF THE THEATRE OF DREAMS
by Iain McCartney
Order via: www.empire-uk.com

Old Trafford endures as a monument to the vision of Manchester United's founder and first patron John Henry Davies. Built during football's first boom, it was originally planned as a 100,000 capacity stadium, and was described as "the most spacious and the most remarkable arena I have ever seen" when it opened in February 1910.

Laterly it has become a world class venue capable of hosting anything from world title boxing fights to rock concerts. To celebrate its centenary, Iain McCartney profiles the construction and re-developments of this legendary venue over the past century complete with previously unpublished photographs and memorabilia.

EMPIRE PUBLICATIONS

Dear Reader,

If you have read this far it's probably safe to say you've enjoyed the book. As the list opposite indicates we are an independent Mancunian publisher specialising in books on the sport, music and history of our great city.

If you would like to receive regular updates on our titles you can join our mailing list by email: **enquiries@empire-uk.com**, by sending your details to: **Empire Publications, 1 Newton St., Manchester M1 1HW** or by calling **0161 872 4721**.

We also update our website regularly: **www.empire-uk.com** with our latest title information.

Cheers

Ashley Shaw
Editor

COMPLETIST'S DELIGHT - THE FULL EMPIRE BACK LIST

ISBN	TITLE	AUTHOR	PRICE	STATUS†
1901746003	SF Barnes: His Life and Times	A Searle	£14.95	IP
1901746011	Chasing Glory	R Grillo	£7.95	IP
190174602X	Three Curries and a Shish Kebab	R Bott	£7.99	IP
1901746038	Seasons to Remember	D Kirkley	£6.95	IP
1901746046	Cups For Cock-Ups+	A Shaw	£8.99	OOP
1901746054	Glory Denied	R Grillo	£8.95	IP
1901746062	Standing the Test of Time	B Alley	£16.95	IP
1901746070	The Encyclopaedia of Scottish Cricket	D Potter	£9.99	IP
1901746089	The Silent Cry	J MacPhee	£7.99	OOP
1901746097	The Amazing Sports Quiz Book	F Brockett	£6.99	IP
1901746100	I'm Not God, I'm Just a Referee	R Entwistle	£7.99	OOP
1901746119	The League Cricket Annual Review 2000	ed. S. Fish	£6.99	IP
1901746143	Roger Byrne - Captain of the Busby Babes	I McCartney	£16.95	OOP
1901746151	The IT Manager's Handbook	D Miller	£24.99	IP
190174616X	Blue Tomorrow	M Meehan	£9.99	IP
1901746178	Atkinson for England	G James	£5.99	IP
1901746186	Think Cricket	C Bazalgette	£6.00	IP
1901746194	The League Cricket Annual Review 2001	ed. S. Fish	£7.99	IP
1901746208	Jock McAvoy - Fighting Legend *	B Hughes	£9.95	IP
1901746216	The Tommy Taylor Story*	B Hughes	£8.99	OOP
1901746224	Willie Pep*+	B Hughes	£9.95	OOP
1901746232	For King & Country*+	B Hughes	£8.95	OOP
1901746240	Three In A Row	P Windridge	£7.99	IP
1901746259	Violet - Life of a legendary goalscorer+PB	R Cavanagh	£16.95	OOP
1901746267	Starmaker	B Hughes	£16.95	IP
1901746283	Morrissey's Manchester	P Gatenby	£5.99	IP
1901746313	Sir Alex, United & Me	A Pacino	£8.99	IP
1901746321	Bobby Murdoch, Different Class	D Potter	£10.99	OOP
190174633X	Goodison Maestros	D Hayes	£5.99	OOP
1901746348	Anfield Maestros	D Hayes	£5.99	OOP
1901746364	Out of the Void	B Yates	£9.99	IP
1901746356	The King - Denis Law, hero of the...	B Hughes	£17.95	OOP
1901746372	The Two Faces of Lee Harvey Oswald	G B Fleming	£8.99	IP
1901746380	My Blue Heaven	D Friend	£10.99	IP
1901746399	Viollet - life of a legendary goalscorer	B Hughes	£11.99	IP
1901746402	Quiz Setting Made Easy	J Dawson	£7.99	IP
1901746410	The Insider's Guide to Manchester United	J Doherty	£20	IP
1901746437	Catch a Falling Star	N Young	£17.95	IP
1901746453	Birth of the Babes	T Whelan	£12.95	OOP
190174647X	Back from the Brink	J Blundell	£10.95	IP
1901746488	The Real Jason Robinson	D Swanton	£17.95	IP
1901746496	This Simple Game	K Barnes	£14.95	IP
1901746518	The Complete George Best	D Phillips	£10.95	IP
1901746526	From Goalline to Touch line	J Crompton	£16.95	IP
1901746534	Sully	A Sullivan	£8.95	IP
1901746542	Memories...	P Hince	£10.95	IP
1901746550	Reminiscences of Manchester	L Hayes	£12.95	IP
1901746569	Morrissey's Manchester - 2nd Ed.	P Gatenby	£8.95	IP
1901746577	Before They Were Famous	C Boujaoude	£10.95	TBP (12/1/10)
1901746585	The Complete Eric Cantona	D Phillips	£10.95	IP
1901746593	18 Times	J Blundell	£9.95	IP

* Originally published by Collyhurst & Moston Lads Club + Out of print PB Superceded by Paperback edition
† In Print/Out Of Print/To Be Published (date)